Retirement Basics

Help for Broke Baby Boomers

Donna Davis

Publisher's Note

The author and publisher have made every effort to ensure that the information in this book was correct at press time. The author and publisher do not assume and hereby disclaim any liability to any party for any loss, damage, or disruption by errors or omissions, whether such errors or omissions result from negligence, accident, or any other cause. Further, the author or publisher does not have any control over and does not assume responsibility for author or third-party websites or their content. This book is not intended as a substitute for medical advice of physicians or other trained medical professionals. The reader should consult with a physician before beginning any weight loss, exercise or other health regiment. This book is not intended as a substitute for professional legal advice. For accurate personal guidance in all matters included herein, the services of a qualified professional should be sought.

First Printing 2014
ISBN 978-0-6923-0337-5
Golden Goddess Press
PO Box 6928
Snowmass Village, CO 81615
www.retirementbasicsforboomers.com

Dedication

*This book is dedicated to the Roman Goddess Abundantia.
May she spill her cornucopia of good fortune, success, and
infinite riches upon each and every one of you.*

TABLE OF CONTENTS

Foreward

Many baby boomers are frozen with fear and have shied away from exploring the basic elements of retirement. This book takes the fear out of looking into what the future holds. It gives an overview of the most important aspects of retiring and how and when benefits are available.

Donna Davis has taken what might be intimidating and confusing procedures and made them easy to understand. She demystifies government red tape and simplifies what you need to know. Donna puts the fundamentals in one place at your fingertips in a streamlined fashion.

In this practical book, you'll find a positive approach to improving your experience with what can often be daunting processes and procedures. Donna helps you to understand the options you have available and gives you the confidence to forge ahead. She imparts first-hand knowledge as she goes through this process herself.

My life's work has been dedicated to understanding and facilitating the progression of the aging process and how it has changed over time. I have spent 40 years envisioning the future with regard to advancing years in individuals, the nation and the world. My company Age

Wave guides Fortune 500 companies and government groups in product and service development for boomers and mature adults.

As a part of my explorations, I have become fascinated with the ongoing transformation of retirement. No longer does retirement necessarily mean that we stop working. It means it's a time for change that may lead to work that stimulates your passion and can even be more fulfilling than your core career.

As a matter of fact, President Jimmy Carter called me one day to ask me for a job. He was pursuing a new venture, and writing a book about the Virtues of Aging. He wanted us to work together. Of course, I agreed and I also asked him to share his spiritual and humanitarian values. Our exchanges had a profound impact on my life.

President Carter is the founder of Habitat for Humanity. He and I have worked side-by-side to help build a family's dream home. It was a very rewarding experience. Donna works with Habitat raising funds by donating furniture from remodeled hotels and lodging. She has been named Habitat's Business Partner of the year in her area for both 2009 and 2012. It's a great cause and I'm pleased to share that interest with her.

Baby boomers changed the world when they came into it and they are changing it as they go out. Aging will never look like it has in the past and requires new ideas and thinking to prepare for what is to come. This book captures the essence of what the next step is all about and conveys it in a positive helpful way. Donna Davis holds your hand and provides enlightening ideas for how to take best advantage of the options about to come your way.

If you'd like to achieve a working knowledge of the approaching aspects of life, this book shares that information in a clear concise manner with warmth and humor. This book is practical, relevant, timely and a great asset to everyone looking ahead to a longer life.

Ken Dychtwald, Ph.D.
Author, *Bodymind, The Age Wave, The Power Years,* and *A New Purpose: Redefining Money, Family, Work, Retirement and Success*
President and CEO, Age Wave

Preface

I set out one morning in 1998 to climb one of Bali's sacred volcanoes, Pura Luhur Lempuyang. The 1700-step climb is a pilgrimage for ordinary Balinese to ask for blessings from above and for assistance with their earthly problems. The pilgrims turned out in their finest. The men wore the traditional gold sarong, crisp white shirt, and a white headdress. The women wore their patterned sarongs with long-sleeved lace tops in a variety of colors making them look like flowers swaying slightly in the wind as they paraded up the stairs.

At a landing near the bottom an old woman was selling sodas out of a washtub. I was surprised because she had Coke, Sprite, and Fanta—an unusual variety for Bali. Out of curiosity I asked how much they were: a couple of thousand rupiah, she said—about a quarter.

Not being accustomed to the confines of the sarong, we Americans slowly climbed the stairs. When we got to the top, there was that same woman. Somehow she had passed us on the steps. Thirsty now, I went over to buy a soda and handed her the money. She shook her head and said that now they were several more thousand rupiah: $1.

Confused, I looked at her and asked why. She gave me an impish grin and said, "Mountain Price." It was brilliant.

In truth, I have lived my entire life at "Mountain Price."

Introduction

"Don't stop, thinking about tomorrow,
Don't stop, it'll soon be here"
—Fleetwood Mac

I always followed the head-in-the-sand retirement plan. After all, it doesn't cost anything and has worked well until now. Now retirement is a reality and for me an uncomfortable one at that.

As I thought about the changes soon to come my way, I realized I knew nothing about the major components of retirement financial existence—Social Security, Medicare, retirement plans. They were a mystery to me. Like it or not, I knew it was time for me to face the future.

The prospect was overwhelming, but I learned all I could. I read government websites, pamphlets, financial articles, and collected an enormous amount of information. The knowledge made me feel confident that I could make informed choices and better decisions for myself.

Like me, millions of baby boomers are not financially prepared for retirement. I imagined there were many of you who felt as wary about the future as I had. So I decided to share my research with the hope that it would ease some of your fears and help you plan a better future.

Retirement Basics is a simple book designed to be an overview of what you need to know for retirement. It's organized so that each chapter is complete unto itself. So feel free to skip around.

While the book thoroughly covers the financial programs that are key to retirement, it also discusses...

- ways to improve your health and decrease your medical expenses,
- the least expensive places to live in the U.S. and abroad,
- techniques to save more and earn more, and
- many other ways to make your retirement comfortable and fun.

Retirement is a time to reinvent yourself, rejuvenate, and stay stimulated. The information in this book will give you the practical tools to do so. Please use it to have a richer, more rewarding retirement life.

Please note: all Websites and song credits are listed at the end of the book.

Chapter 1

Social Security

"We can work it out"
— The Beatles

Hard to believe that we baby boomers have reached or are approaching retirement age. The reality is difficult for many to digest, and it's easy to try to avoid knowing the facts, because then we feel we can hold off the inevitable. But, it's time to take our heads out of the sand.

Approaching our golden years might be something many of us do not want to face, but waiting to learn the facts is not going to change the situation. Knowing what lies ahead can influence decisions that may make a big difference in what you have to live on during your retirement.

Let's start with Social Security.

First of all, remember that this is your money. It was taken out of your paycheck every week. *You earned it,* and you are just being paid back for what you contributed. Never feel bad and never let anyone make you feel bad about claiming what is rightfully yours.

Social Security is going to be a blessing to many of us, and it may help us out in tough circumstances and a bad economy. Rather than guess, it is wise to find out exactly how big a blessing it will be for you. I know the Social Security Administration (SSA) is a government agency and just the sound of it may bring visions of tedious paperwork and red tape, but it's really not that scary.

Social Security has a number of online tools to make finding information easy for you. You can apply online, get your individual statement, and get most if not all of your questions answered without a visit. Take advantage of what they have to offer. It is much better to know for sure what you can expect to receive and plan accordingly.

The earliest age for a worker to begin collecting Social Security is 62, and many people do in fact choose this option. If you do start collecting early, you will receive a lower monthly amount for the duration, which is until you die.

Another collection option is to wait until you reach your "Full Retirement Age" (FRA) which is determined by the year you were born. Until 1983, 65 was the full retirement age for everybody. Then Congress changed the law, and now we all have to work longer. For most baby boomers, FRA is between the ages of 66 and 67. You can find your exact Full Retirement Age by using the link above. If you choose to wait until your FRA to collect, the amount of your monthly payment will be considerably more. If you wait until age 70, it will go up even further. Here's how it works.

According to the Social Security Retirement Planner, "if you begin collecting benefits at age 62, your monthly benefit amount is reduced by about 30 percent. The amount reduced decreases the longer you wait. The reduction for starting benefits at age:

- 63 is about 25 percent;

- 64 is about 20 percent;

- 65 is about 13.3 percent; and

- 66 is about 6.7 percent."

The percentage will vary depending on your Full Retirement age. Therefore, you may see other amounts listed in different sources.

Another way to look at this is that for each year you wait to collect between age 62 and your Full Retirement Age, your benefit increases. Once you reach your Full Retirement Age, you collect what is considered 100 percent of your benefit. If you decide *not* to begin collecting at your FRA, you receive what are known as Delayed Retirement Credits. For every year you postpone collecting, after you have reached your FRA, you receive an 8 percent increase in your payment amount. After you reach age 70, you do not receive any additional increase in your benefits. Therefore, there is no reason to wait any longer to begin collecting Social Security.

Worth noting: You can begin collecting Social Security at age 62. However, Medicare coverage begins at age 65. You will need to have an alternate source of health insurance until you are 65.

I always thought that everybody collecting Social Security got the same monthly amount. I thought it was a set amount, but that is not the case. The payment will be different for everybody and is dependent on how much you have put into the system over your working lifetime.

You contribute 6.2 percent of your earnings in Social Security Tax up to $117,000. Your employer matches that with an additional 6.2 percent. So your contributions are dependent on what your earnings have been over your working lifetime. It can be challenging to calculate your exact benefit because your estimated award is calculated not only on your past contributions, but also on your future earnings and at what age you choose to begin collecting benefits.

Here's the gist of how your benefits are calculated. You need a total of 40 credits over your lifetime to receive Social

Security retirement benefits. You earn up to four credits per year through your work. For each $1,200 you earn one credit. Once you have earned $4,800 you have earned your four credits for the year. Now that you have enough credits, SSA will take your 35 highest earning years, convert them to today's dollars, put them into a formula and calculate your benefit. The 35 highest-earning years become important if you are still working. Not only are you increasing your benefit by working longer, you may also be increasing your benefit by having more years at a higher income.

SSA used to mail out a statement to potential recipients annually. They no longer do that, but you can see your individual statement by going to ssa.gov and clicking on "My Social Security." You can then create a personal account and you will be able to view and print your own statement with a complete list of your yearly earnings over your working life and your estimated benefits at this point in time. You can also call the Social Security number 800-772-1213 and use the automated system to obtain your statement.

The current maximum monthly benefit amount at Full Retirement Age is $2,642. To achieve this, you must have an income of $117,000 or higher for 35 years. (Makes me wish I'd worked a little harder.)

If you don't want to open an account, you can use the benefit estimator to determine your approximate benefits. I found the statement and the estimator to be nearly identical. However, one advantage of the estimator is that you can put in various yearly earnings amounts for the future, whereas the statement assumes you will be making the same amount you are now until you apply for benefits. So, if you are going to be earning more over the next several years than you are now, your benefit will increase and the estimator can show you by how much.

As an example, I am 58 years old and how many more years I work and how much I make in the future changes the benefit greatly.

As per my Social Security Statement, I will receive $1,423 per month if I begin collecting at 62. My payment would be $2,043 at FRA and $2,700 at 70. If I put in an arbitrary salary into the Social Security Estimator, here's what I found.

With what I have contributed, if I work until I am 62 (four more years) at my current salary, my benefit would be $1,423/month. If I work until 62 and make $150,000 per year until then (wishful thinking), my benefit goes up to $1,522. At my FRA with the higher income, it goes up to $2,142, and at 70 it goes up to $2,988.

This is to give you an idea of the significant difference timing and the amount of future earnings has on the payment you will receive. You can use the estimator to help you make decisions on whether or not working for a longer period is worth it for you. You can also determine if it will be beneficial to take a higher paying job to get an increased payment. It can also show you that you may want to take a lower paying, less stressful job because the payment amounts may not be that different.

So you can see there are many variables involved in determining just how much you will receive. You can increase your benefit by waiting longer to begin collecting payments or by increasing your income in the last few years before you retire. The government does assist in increasing your benefit. You get periodic cost of living increases. Another possibility to the change in your benefit is a change in the law by Congress. This is the most frightening of all and should be monitored very closely by all retirees. With many of us struggling, this is no time for any kind of decrease in benefits.

One thing to note is that Social Security checks are a thing of the past. I remember my grandfather waiting by the mailbox on "check day." When his check was due, it was an event, something he looked forward to. Even when he moved from his house to an apartment, he'd pace in the lobby of his building with the other retirees until he had that check in hand. There was a physical connection, a process to getting the check, taking it to the bank, filling out the slip, and depositing it.

Well, there are no more checks. There's automatic deposit or a reloadable debit card. I feel a little bad because we won't have that excitement that comes from getting a check, but maybe we're used to it. I had my tax refund deposited automatically for the first time this year and it was a non-event, just a change in numbers on the computer screen. I didn't get that fun feeling when you see the colored paper and the Statue of Liberty peeking through the window in the envelope, but that's the tradeoff for not having to worry about lost or stolen checks.

All payments go directly into your bank account or are added to your government issued debit card. From what I understand, it is better to have it put in the bank. If any funds are lost or stolen from your accounts, the bank can reimburse you. With the federal government, you have to prove you haven't made the charges to your card. It may be harder and take longer to get your money back.

When the payments do come, Social Security will mean different things for each individual. For some it will be the only income you have for retirement. For others it may be a boost to a pension, 401(k) plan, investment portfolio, or savings. Because of these differences, people make different choices as to when to start collecting. This will be the biggest decision you will have to make with regards to receiving your Social Security benefits.

There are several options available and it's important to know what is right for you.

Let's take a look. Should you decide to take benefits at age 62, you can continue to work, but there's a catch. There's a limit to how much you can make before it affects your payment amount. For 2014, the yearly amount you can earn without decreasing your benefit is $15,480. If you make more than that, the government will deduct $1 from your payment for every $2 you earn above the maximum. If you want to keep working, you will have to figure out if it is worth collecting early.

Once you reach Full Retirement Age, your benefits will not be reduced if you continue to work, regardless of the amount you make. The benefits can, however, be taxed.

Should you choose to begin collecting at FRA, Social Security recommends contacting them at the beginning of that year. The website says, "Even if you are still working, you may be able to receive some or all of your benefits for the months before you reach FRA." It is a good idea to get things started and ready to go whether you receive additional benefits or not.

Most financial management companies recommend that you wait until age 70 to begin collecting your benefits. At that age, your payments will be at the maximum and there is no benefit to waiting past this point. The majority of people cannot afford to wait that long. In order to do that you will need another source of income sufficient to cover all of your expenses until that time.

Many people would like to wait for this option, but often it's not feasible. They are forced to apply for Social Security benefits earlier for various reasons. They may have lost their job or are no longer able to work. They, or a family member, may have become ill and required care. There are numerous reasons for not waiting until age 70 to begin collecting. Then there are those of us who just don't want to work anymore and there's no crime in that.

Assume that the next 10-20 years are going to be the best you have left in your life. That's not a pleasant thought, but still worth thinking about. Many feel they don't want to spend these years working. If you wait to retire until 66 or 70, you may not be fit or able enough to do the things you want to do. Some people would like to enjoy their grandchildren while they are growing up; they'd like to engage in their favorite pastimes like golf or fishing, or do some traveling. They feel that they've worked long and hard and should enjoy life while they can.

My friend, Don, chose to apply for SSA benefits at age 62 and it worked out well for him. He's a ski bum in Aspen, one of the costliest but coolest places to live in the U.S. I have to hand it to him. Don is an ex-Marine and is now in his 70s. He has made his life work while collecting the lowest benefit possible for him, the only guaranteed income he had. Even though Aspen is a wealthy town, it does have affordable housing for workers. Don is a very talented handyman and woodworker. He was able to get work in the off-seasons repairing and touching up high-end condo units before the next season began. Working just a few months out of the year, he kept his income under the maximum allowed for Social Security. It also made him eligible for housing, which brought his rent for a one-bedroom apartment to about $800 a month. This includes all utilities. Prior to that, he lived with a roommate in a 2-bedroom, 2-bath apartment within walking distance of the slopes for $700.

Don has quite the life. He skis all winter and hikes all summer. He's tall, handsome, *and* a great skier. He's easy to spot on the slopes with his silver hair and color-coordinated outfits. All of his ski gear is a perfect blend of red, white, and black. He always looks well put together.

He also knows everybody in town and is out socializing just about every night of the week. He doesn't spend much on food, watches his budget, and so he is able to live a great life in a spectacular place on a single Social Security check and part-time work alone.

I'm not saying it's easy, but it can be done. Many communities have senior housing and discounts that can make a big difference in your cost of living. Knowing what you have coming in—and what discounts are available to you—allows you to make good choices and in many cases live a better life.

Most of us don't want to think about this, but a key factor in planning retirement is estimating how long you are going to live. Death can be a taboo and difficult subject in many families, but not always. When we talked about death with my friend's mom, she always said she wanted to be "shot by a jealous lover at 92."

Excluding all bullets, what do you see in your future? Do people in your family have a long life expectancy? Are they healthy?

Longevity is a major factor in the choices you make for collecting your benefits. You need to get out your crystal ball and think about how long you will need to provide for yourself. Though just an educated guess, longevity is something we need to seriously consider.

To help us out there are longevity estimators to determine your approximate life span. They only consider your current age and gender without allowing for your family or medical history, which are factors you should keep in mind because they can change the outcome greatly.

You must think about this objectively. My estimate said I would live until I was 86.5. My grandfather lived till 91 and my great grandmother until 94. Like it or not, I might be around for a long time.

This is so important in planning, because you need to consider how long your money needs to last. While Social Security has a set amount for each individual at various ages, how long you will live helps you choose which retirement age is best for you—and when you will need the money most. What it comes down to is this: do you want a smaller benefit for a longer time, or a larger benefit for a shorter time?

Here's what I mean. Please keep in mind these are approximate numbers estimating a lifespan of 86.5 years.

If I begin collecting at age 62, my total lifetime benefit will be $418,362.

If I begin collecting at Full Retirement Age of 66 and four months my lifetime benefit will be $526,932.

If I wait till age 70, my total lifetime benefit will be $591,624.

The breakeven point where waiting pays off is about 80 years old. A woman's estimated life span is 86.5 and a man's is 84. If a person of either sex files at age 70 and dies before 80, they will not have gotten the most out of his or her benefits and perhaps worked longer than they needed to.

I am not suggesting you try to get the maximum amount out of the government, but look for the best time and amount for you to live on and enjoy your life.

Don't forget Social Security payments stop upon your death. Uncollected amounts are *not* passed on as part of your estate. They remain in the general pool. Your family will *not* collect any funds left on the table.

Social Security has many services available that will help you figure it all out, to the extent possible, for free. Beware of the many ads online and in the mail that will target you to process your paperwork for a fee. There's no need for any of these services when you are entitled to advice for nothing. True government websites usually have .gov or .org in the address.

Windfalls and Loopholes

Please note there are two laws that can affect the amount of your benefit. One is the Windfall Elimination Provision, and the other is the Government Pension Offset. If you receive a government pension these are the two laws you need to be aware of.

My sister-in-law, Lynda, a widow, resigned from her teaching job at age 62. She worked in the State of Kentucky for 18 years. Prior to that she taught and worked at various jobs in New York for 24 years. Each year she received a notice from Social Security telling her how much she would receive if she retired at certain ages. Being a teacher, she had a set pension that she would also receive from the state of Kentucky.

She went to the Social Security office with paper in hand expecting to get the $1,305 a month they quoted. In Kentucky, some government workers do not pay into Social Security, but Lynda had worked in New York and contributed from there for so many years; according to her statement she was entitled to collect those benefits. But there is something called the Windfall Elimination Provision: if you are a government worker entitled to a pension, and you contributed to Social Security at another job, you are *not* eligible for the full Social Security amount generally awarded for your contribution.

Lynda receives just $435 a month, not the $1,305 she was expecting. There is a formula used, but essentially she is receiving one-third of the amount expected and one-third of the amount Social Security told her she would get. (Apparently the federal and state governments don't talk to each other.) No one ever told her she would lose any part of her rightful benefits. She was stunned. She'd just gone from thinking she would have a comfortable retirement to having to scrimp and watch every penny.

She lost $870 a month for life. If she lives to be 82, twenty years from her retirement date that will amount to $208,800 gone for good.

The Government Pension Offset is similar but pertains to individuals collecting Social Security benefits under the spousal, widow, or widower provisions. If you have your own government pension and did not pay into Social Security and are also entitled to spousal, widow, or widower Social Security benefits, those benefits may be reduced by as much as two-thirds of your pension.

I mention this as an alert in case there are some, like Lynda, in this position that are not aware of it. Don't get caught by surprise. Check with your Human Resource Department at work, a local tax accountant, or your local Social Security office. Lay out all of your information and ask questions well in advance. You can then base your decisions on fact and perhaps avoid some heartache.

Lynda has figured out a way to make it work. It took some time, but with tutoring jobs and cutting expenses, she is enjoying her retirement. As a matter of fact, she just got back from a cruise—with an off-season discount, of course.

Social Security for Married Couples

It doesn't take a genius to figure out that two incomes are better than one, but it may take one to figure out the best time for each of the two parties of a married couple to apply for their benefits.

In fact, there are 81different scenarios that can help a couple maximize the amount of their payments. The difference can mean well over $100,000 in the course of lifetime benefits. It can also mean a big difference in your income at different times during your retirement.

In most married couples today, each partner has worked enough to earn his or her own benefits. Each party can begin collecting benefits independently of their spouse any time after the age of 62. However, thinking about this jointly is the right idea.

It may be valuable for a couple to apply for the benefits of the lower-earning spouse *earlier* and wait to take the benefits for the higher earner at age 70. This would give the couple the maximum monthly income of the higher earner for the later years in their lives.

Worth noting: upon the death of one spouse, the surviving spouse is able to keep receiving only one benefit. You would, of course, receive the higher of the two and if you are able, it is best to have one earner's benefit be as high as possible. This would insure that the living spouse gets the most possible income when they are getting a single monthly check. It can be a challenge to go from two incomes to one, particularly at such a difficult period in life. You can do your best to maximize your income and prepare for this time. Women generally live longer and, in most cases, the husband is the higher earner. So, beefing up the husband's benefit may be in her best interest.

Which of the many Social Security options a married couple chooses will depend solely upon their individual circumstances, how long they have worked, and how much they have contributed over their lifetimes. It will be important whether or not they will continue to work and if they have enough funds to be able to wait longer to apply for the second benefit. Your assets, tax brackets, and dependents will also play a part. Social Security can help you through the process. There is also software available to assist with this decision.

Spousal Benefits

Spousal benefits were designed to provide income to a spouse who has either *not* contributed into the Social Security system or has not earned enough to qualify for a large benefit. In both cases the lower earner can collect on a spouse's contribution. The maximum award will be 50 percent of the major earner's payment amount.

You are entitled to spousal benefits if you have been married for at least one year or are divorced and had been married for at least ten years. In both situations you must be at least 62 years of age to apply.

If you *have* reached full retirement age, you may receive 50 percent of the amount of your spouse's benefit. Your spouse must be Full Retirement Age and must have applied for Social Security benefits.

Your spouse may elect to suspend payments so that Delayed Retirement Credits continue to increase his or her benefit amount. However, as your spouse's benefit increases, yours does not.

If you are FRA and eligible for spousal benefits, you may also apply for benefits on your own record and suspend payment. The benefit on your record will continue to increase until you reach age 70, when it would be at its maximum. You can then elect to receive the higher of the two for future payments.

Only one of you can collect spousal benefits.

If you *have not* reached Full Retirement Age and *do not* have enough credits on your own record to receive benefits, you can apply for spousal support. Your spouse must be Full Retirement Age and must have applied for Social Security benefits. Since you are applying early, your benefit will be reduced in a manner similar to that of an individual. It may be reduced up to 30 percent depending on your age when you apply. For example, if your spouse's benefit is $2,000 per month, at Full Retirement Age your benefit would be $1,000. If you apply at age 62, your benefit will be about $700.

If you *have not* reached Full Retirement Age and *do* have enough credits on your own record to be eligible for benefits, Social Security will pay that amount first. If what you would receive as a spousal benefit is more than what you will receive on your own record, you will get a combination of the two benefits to equal the higher amount.

For example, if your spousal benefit would be $1,000 per month and the amount you would receive on your own record is $600, you would be paid $600 on your own record and $400 in spousal benefits for a total of $1,000.

If the amount you would receive on your own record is higher than what you would receive in spousal benefits, you will *not* be eligible for spousal benefits.

If you are divorced and had been married to that person for at least ten years, you may be entitled to collect a spousal benefit on your previous husband or wife's contribution. You must be unmarried, at least 62, and your former spouse must be eligible for benefits as well. In this case your former spouse does not have to apply for benefits for you to be eligible, and your award does not affect his or hers at all. Unlike married couples, both individuals of a divorced couple can collect spousal support on each other's record.

Once you apply for this benefit, the amount of your payment does not change, even if your former partner's award goes up, yours does not.

Same-Sex Couples

As of June 2013, the Social Security Administration provides spousal and survivor benefits to same- sex couples. If you are in a same-sex marriage or other legal union, you may be eligible for benefits. You are encouraged to apply for any benefits you feel you might be entitled to right away. The Social Security Administration states: "We continue to work closely with the Department of Justice. In the coming weeks and months we will develop and implement additional policy and processing instructions."

If you are married, separated, divorced, or a survivor, you may be eligible to receive benefits. This is a great step forward. Find out what you may be entitled to.

***

Spousal benefits are some of the options that you may want to consider when planning your future. Once you apply, Social Security will review your application. If they feel you could get a higher benefit by applying in another way, they should contact you. They will not, however, tell you when to apply and that can be the most important decision. Once the time has passed, you cannot go back and collect for any missed opportunity. Therefore, it is wise to have a well-thought-out plan early in the game.

Talk with Social Security as many times as you need to. Talk with your accountant and get specific information on your financial status. Most importantly, talk with each other. You'll be surprised at how many couples do not approach this together and, therefore, may be missing out on funds that could make them much more comfortable as they age.

There are many options, but only you can choose which is best. Considering the different scenarios can help maximize the amount you receive as a couple and, for the unmarried, divorced person, how much you receive as an individual over your lifetime. You want to get the most you are entitled to at the time you need it most. You never know what may happen in life, and you need to be as prepared as possible for the unexpected. Think it over, talk to the right people, and make the best choice for you.

Survivor Benefits

It can be personally and financially devastating to lose a loved one particularly if he or she is the major provider for your family. Social Security not only provides benefits for retirees, but also for a worker's family. Widows, widowers, children, and dependent parents may be eligible for survivor benefits. The amount of the benefit depends on the contributions of the worker and the age at which he or she died.

The surviving spouse can apply for benefits at 60 years of age, but at a reduced rate. At FRA, he or she is entitled to 100 percent of the worker's benefit. Also, the benefit is subject to an earnings limit and should you continue to work and exceed the maximum allowable amount, your benefit may be reduced as well.

A surviving divorced spouse may also be entitled to benefits if he or she was married for at least ten years and is age 60 or older. Applying for this benefit does not affect the amount other family members may receive including children or a current spouse of the deceased.

Dependent parents may also qualify for benefits. The parent must be 62 or older, and the worker must have provided at least 50 percent of the parent's support.

If you are currently receiving spousal benefits, you will get a higher amount by applying for *survivor* benefits. Spousal benefits are at 50 percent, and survivor benefits are at 100 percent of the worker's benefit. You must report the death and provide a death certificate to Social Security to make this change.

Widows or widowers cannot get survivor benefits if they remarry before the age of 60. If they remarry after 60, they can still collect benefits on their deceased spouse's work record. It may be beneficial to postpone marriage if your survivor award is larger than the award on your own record, or a spousal award on your new partner's record.

Widows, widowers, and children are entitled to a one-time, lump-sum benefit of $255. Other survivors are not. You need to apply for this benefit.

Scenarios to Consider

As discussed, there are many alternatives for you to choose from. The most common are that each individual in a couple files for his or her own benefit when they turn 62 and receive that benefit for life. Both may also wait until Full Retirement Age to apply for benefits and receive a higher benefit for life.

Another choice is that one person files for benefits early and the second waits until FRA or later to file to increase the benefit over time. If we include spousal benefits, it is often common for the eldest to apply for benefits and suspend payment so that the younger spouse can collect on spousal benefits. Then the benefit of the elder spouse increases over time and provides a higher award later in life.

The most critical factor in deciding which is best for you will be how much income you need today. It may look very attractive to wait and collect a higher benefit, but it may not be possible if you cannot survive without the income right now.

Seek help in making these decisions. Often individuals, like me, with a limited amount of money, feel that it is not worth it to hire a financial planner or pay a tax accountant. You may feel you don't have enough to worry about. On the other hand, you may be the one who needs it most. Your future depends on making a good decision. There are also many local organizations aside from SSA that provide financial services to seniors for free or a reduced rate. Seek them out and take advantage of what they have to offer. It could make an incredible difference in what you have now and in the future.

How to Apply

When you are ready, you can apply online, by phone, or in person.

To apply online go to <u>ssa.gov.</u> Click on "My Social Security" and create a personal account. Open the application. It takes about 15 minutes to complete. You do not have to finish it all at once. You can save it and come back. Once completed, you will be given an application number so that you can check the status at any time.

Before you start, it is helpful to know your Full Retirement Age, how your benefits will be reduced if you retire early, the maximum amount you can earn if you work, and your life expectancy. If you are registering for direct deposit, have your bank information handy, too.

Once submitted, Social Security will check your application and contact you if they need more information. They should also let you know if they think you can receive more money by applying in a different way. When the process is complete, they will send you a letter by snail mail.

Don't like computers? No problem! You can call 800-772-1213 to get all the information you need. You will be asked identifying questions before being put through; don't be intimidated. There may be a wait when you call this number, but there is an option to get a call back. Your call is put in the queue, and when an agent is available they will return your call. (They have caller ID, and they know your number.) They tell you approximately how long it will take for someone to call you. On a Tuesday the wait was 55 minutes and on a Thursday the wait was 26 minutes. The return call was received within a few minutes of the estimated time. When they did call, they asked if I was ready or would I prefer a call in ten minutes. If you're in the middle of something and can't take the call, you don't lose your place in line. (I thought this system worked well.)

To apply by phone call the same number as above 800-772-1213. You can make an appointment to complete your application. An agent will fill it out with you and guide you through the process. You can do it all from the comfort of your home.

While speaking to the agent, if you prefer to apply in person, you can ask for the location and number of your local office. You can also find this information online. To find the office closest to you, go to ssa.gov and search location, enter your zip code, and click "locate." You will be directed to the appropriate location and given the phone number to reach that particular office. Office hours are listed, and a map with detailed directions is available.

I had more of a challenge calling my local office. If the wait is longer than 15 minutes, it is suggested you call back at another time, and the call is disconnected. After three attempts, I did get put in the queue, and the call was answered in 14 minutes. I imagine there is a concentration of calls due to the shortened office hours. Be persistent.

When you get through at your local office, you can make an appointment to process your application with an agent either in person or over the phone.

I visited the office in Glenwood Springs, Colorado, to see what it was like. I didn't have an appointment. I waited only 15 minutes before having all of my questions pleasantly answered by an agent. I was very happy I went and personally saw what it was like. Social Security offices have had their hours cut. The Glenwood office is open Monday, Wednesday, and Friday. I went on a Wednesday, and it was open from 9am-12pm. (Check the hours before stopping by.)

I thought the experience in a big city might be different than the one in rural Colorado. So, on a recent trip to New

York, I visited the Social Security office there. I was pleasantly surprised when things were just about the same.

Fear Not

Now we know a little bit more about Social Security and now you have the tools to calculate your estimated benefits and make educated decisions about your future. The Social Security Administration is there to help you and has a multitude of resources to make this process as easy as possible for you. Social Security is a wonderful benefit that can get us through our retirement if we understand our options and their consequences, we plan well, and we use all the resources available to us.

In an effort to provide you with the most up-to-date information, I have visited many websites and read many articles and pamphlets. I've spoken to and visited Social Security administrators for clarification. I have read a lot of conflicting information and have tried to verify everything said here to the best of my ability. But, I ask you to please check any information here with the appropriate agency and within the confines of your particular circumstance.

This book is meant only as an overview of the system in general. Investigate your particular situation fully and make knowledgeable decisions based on current facts. I wish you the best financial outcome and a happy retirement.

Chapter 2

Medicare

"A B C, easy as 1 2 3
As simple as do re mi"
—The Jackson 5

Medicare is a national health insurance program covering workers 65 or older who have paid Medicare taxes into the system. In most cases if you are 65 and eligible for Social Security, you will be eligible for Medicare. You must have been a legal resident of the United States for at least five consecutive years and have paid into the system for at least ten years. If you qualify, Medicare is provided regardless of current income or pre-existing medical history.

If you are eligible for Medicare, your enrollment in Part A and Part B should be automatic. You should receive a Medicare card in the mail three months before you turn 65. If you are enrolling after your initial eligibility at 65, or have not paid into the system, you must enroll between January 1 and March 31. Once enrolled, your coverage will automatically renew every year unless you generate changes.

Worth noting: You can begin collecting Social Security at age 62. However, Medicare coverage does not begin until age 65. You will need to have an alternate source of health insurance until you are 65.

The funds for Medicare come from a separate payroll tax and not from the Social Security pool. Employees pay 1.4 percent of their income, and the employer matches that.

Medicare has no limit on your income. No matter how much you make, you are taxed on the entire amount.

Like Social Security, you have paid into the Medicare system your entire working life. You paid to ensure you had medical care as you aged. You have paid for this service in advance, and you are entitled to it.

On average Medicare covers about 48 percent of your health care costs. You will be responsible for the difference with deductibles, co-pays, and out-of-pocket expenses for uncovered services. This can add up to quite a bit. Medicare does not cover long-term hospital care. It does, however, cover hospice care.

Should you leave the country temporarily or decide to live overseas, you will not have Medicare insurance. Medicare covers you only when you are in the United States or its territories. You will have to make other arrangements for your health care needs outside the country. Should you return to the U.S., you can apply once you have established residency.

Medicare publishes a booklet, _Medicare and You_, annually. You can download it electronically or request a printed copy. It provides the most up-to-date information and an overview of all of the components of Medicare coverage.

There are a few different parts to Medicare coverage, and each will cover a certain type of care, but there is some crossover so you will need to check with your doctor or hospital to find out the rules and regulations specific to your condition(s).

Part A

Part A generally covers hospital care, surgeries, home health services, and hospice. For hospital care coverage to kick in, you must have a stay that crosses two midnights. (Sounds a little like the movie "Twilight" doesn't it?) The time before a patient spends two nights is generally covered by Part B. I told you it can be tricky. Most people do not pay for Part A. There is no premium. If you are not eligible for it for free, you can purchase a policy. There is a deductible of $1,216 for everyone for each benefit period and coinsurance for hospital stays of 60 days or longer.

Part A also covers you if you are in a skilled nursing facility for physical or occupational therapy. Speech and language therapy, as well as medications and equipment while an inpatient are also covered. There may be limits to the amount of therapy you are able to receive. Part A also includes ambulance transportation to and from the hospital.

Several years ago my grandfather had a massive heart attack. Knowing he was having a heart attack, he got into his car and drove himself to the hospital. I couldn't believe it, and when I asked him why he didn't call 911, he said it was because the ambulance wasn't covered by his insurance. I'm very happy to see Medicare Part A covers transportation. We do not need these people on the road. It's enough to give *me* a heart attack.

Part B

Part B is optional. You will be automatically enrolled in Part B with Part A when you reach age 65. You should receive your card three months before your 65th birthday. You will also receive instructions on how to reject Part B should you not wish to participate.

Part B coverage includes doctor visits, x-rays, vaccinations, most outpatient hospital procedures, and laboratory and diagnostic tests.

Most people currently pay a premium of $104.90 per month. The charge will be automatically deducted from your Social Security payment. This makes it very convenient. There is an annual deductible of $147 for everyone. After that is met, Medicare generally pays 80 percent of most physician services. You will be responsible for paying the additional 20 percent as coinsurance.

Medicare Part B does *not* have a maximum out-of-pocket amount. Unlike most insurance policies, there is no cap to the sum you may have to pay. If you require repeated doctor visits and treatment, no matter how large the bill, you are still responsible for at least 20 percent of the payment.

This is where a Medigap policy comes in. We'll discuss that below.

Medicare Part B does cover canes, walkers, scooters, prosthetics, oxygen, and other necessary medical equipment. Dental, eyeglasses, and hearing aids are *not* covered. Regulations can change and you would normally be notified when they are, but just in case, I suggest you check with Medicare *before* purchasing any of these items. If you have any questions regarding your coverage, I suggest you contact Medicare directly.

If you delay signing up for Part B when you turn 65 and enroll at a later date, you will be charged a permanent 10 percent increase in payments. This does not apply if you are currently employed and covered by another policy. Once you do stop working, you have a window of eight months to begin your Medicare coverage penalty free. This does *not* include COBRA.

Part C

Part C, the Medicare Advantage Plan, is also optional and operates like an HMO (Health Maintenance Organization) or a PPO (Preferred Provider Organization).

Part C includes both Part A (hospital insurance) and Part B (medical insurance), so you do not have to register for those separately. You do still need to pay the Part B premium. The coverage in Part C is provided by Medicare-approved private companies and in general you must use the providers included in your particular plan. There is a premium in addition to the one you pay for Part B. This covers you for services *not* covered under Part A or Part B. You are required to pay any deductibles, coinsurance, and costs for non-covered services. Costs and coverage vary by individual plan, and there are many different ones available. Choose your policy carefully as you can only change once a year. The enrollment period for Part C runs from October 15 to February 14.

Medigap

Medigap, Medicare Supplemental Insurance, is in addition to Part A and Part B. Medigap covers co-pays, deductibles, and other costs that Medicare may not. It fills the "gap." It may also cover services received while outside the country.

Medigap plans are provided by private companies and are not connected to Part C. You will pay a monthly premium in addition to your Medicare Part B payment.

You must be enrolled in Part A and Part B to qualify for Medigap. Forms are first submitted to Medicare, which pays its portion to the provider. Claims are then sent to the Medigap company which pays the remainder for covered services. Not all services are covered. Again, dental, eyeglasses and hearing aids may not be included.

Costs vary greatly depending on the company but are generally in the neighborhood of $125-$175 per month per person. This coverage is supplemented to make the policies more affordable. If you are married, each spouse will need to buy his or her own policy. Medigap does not provide spousal coverage. If you have a Medicare Advantage Plan (Part C), you may not participate in a Medigap plan.

Medigap can only be provided by <u>companies approved by Medicare</u>. Not every insurance company qualifies. You may work for a company whose policy is not approved and doesn't work with the Medicare system. You can still use it instead of Medicare until you stop working, but do not have to. You can transfer to Medicare once you reach age 65. Many do so because the coverage from Medicare is less expensive.

Part D

Part D is a prescription drug program. Anyone with Part A or Part B is eligible. To receive prescription drug coverage, you must enroll in a separate plan. *Medicare does not offer Part D plans.* These plans are approved and regulated by Medicare, but are administered by private companies. "Plans choose which drugs (or even classes of drugs) they wish to cover, at what level (or tier) they wish to cover it, and are free to choose *not* to cover some drugs at all." There are standards that these companies must comply with, but the coverage can still vary widely.

If you have enrolled in Part C, you should be able to get prescription drug coverage through your HMO or PPO. You cannot purchase a policy through Part D.

Medicare offers the <u>Medicare Plan Finder</u> to help you find the prescription drug plan that is best for you. You will need to enter all of the drugs you take, the dosages, and frequency. Medicare will then generate a list of plans in your area that cover your prescriptions.

When I entered my information, I got a list of 32 plans. Policy premiums and deductibles were included. There was also a rating next to each plan, indicating Medicare's satisfaction level with the company. This is great because it can narrow down your choices and help avoid a costly, possibly unpleasant experience.

You can enter the policy price range. Then you only have to review those that meet your qualifications.

The costs for premiums vary widely, as does the coverage. The average price per month is about $60. There are some policies listed as high as $300 per month and some as low as $12. The deductibles range from $0 to $310, which is the maximum allowed. Most have a 25 percent co-pay for each prescription.

The low-cost plans are subsidized, and you will need to qualify for them. Medicare has a program called Extra Help that assists low-income individuals with prescription drug costs. Participants save an average of $3,900 per year. You can apply online.

The Medicare Savings Program (MSP) can direct you to the requirements for your individual state for help with your Prescription Drug Plan. If you qualify, it may also pay your Part A and Part B premiums.

As we have seen Medicare is a great benefit that provides health care coverage for those over 65. The program was designed to bring medical care to seniors at an affordable rate. The idea was that all American workers should be entitled to quality health care.

In general, as we age, we have more conditions that need medical care. For many of us, this is also the time where our income is lower and when we need the help. We have paid for this service in advance to insure we receive quality care as we age. Medicare is in place so that those of us who contributed can be comfortable in knowing that we will be taken care of.

Chapter 3

Supplemental Security Income

*"When you're down and troubled
and you need a helping hand"*
—James Taylor

You may be eligible for <u>Supplemental Security Income</u> (SSI), if you are over 65 and your income is low.

Social Security and Supplemental Security Income are often confused. They are two completely different programs, and the funds come from two completely different sources. Social Security is our country's system of retirement benefits for workers. Employees pay a percentage of their salary into a fund, which is reimbursed to them later in life to ensure they have income as they age. Social Security is money that has been earned by the worker, money returned to them to make retirement more financially stable and comfortable.

SSI is a public assistance program designed for those in need because they have a very low income and have trouble paying for the basic necessities in life. With Social Security you can have $1 million in the bank and still collect your award: after all, rich or poor, it is *your* money. With SSI you must prove you are living at about or below poverty level, and if you earn more than the designated amount, you lose your benefits. It is important, *extremely* important, not to confuse these two programs. Each has a very distinct purpose and function.

It can be confusing because SSI is managed by the Social Security Administration, even though the funds come from different sources. Be assured that this public assistance program is not depleting funds in the general Social Security pool. The money comes from the General Tax Revenue.

It is advantageous for the recipient to have both programs managed by the same agency because receiving one benefit (SSA) will affect your eligibility for the other (SSI). You may be able to get both Social Security and SSI depending on your individual circumstances. The amount of one affects the other and having all of your information in one place helps you not have to duplicate your efforts. It becomes a streamlined and easier process.

The average Social Security monthly payment amount in 2014 is $1,294, and the maximum earnings allowable for SSI is $1,527. This means that many people collecting Social Security may also be eligible for SSI. Do yourself a favor and investigate whether or not you qualify, especially if Social Security is your only income during your retirement years.

Here are more of the specifics. You may be eligible to receive SSI if you are over 65, and your income is low. You must be a U.S. Citizen or National and live in the United States. These benefits are based on need, not on past earnings, and are financed by General Tax Revenue. Both your income and resources are evaluated to determine your eligibility.

According to the Federal SSI website, the maximum monthly earnings you can have to collect SSI must be less than $1,527. For a couple the maximum earnings is $2,249, but all of your income is not included when deciding if you qualify for SSI—including "the first $20 per month you receive in income; the first $65 per month you earn from working; anything you gain from Supplemental Nutrition Assistance Program, SNAP, (formerly known as Food Stamps); and most home energy assistance."

In general, your resources can't be over $2,000 for an individual or $3,000 for a couple. Resources may include "real estate, bank accounts, cash, stocks, or bonds."

Remember that many of your resources are *not* included in this determination. For example, "your home and the land it is on; life insurance policies with a face value of less than $1,500; your car (usually); burial plots; and up to $1,500 in burial funds."

As you can see, there are many variables at play here. If you are anywhere in the ballpark of eligibility, make sure to investigate. Let SSI figure it out for you. Do not assume, even if you earn or have more than the maximum amounts listed, that you do not qualify. That money could make a big difference in the quality of your life.

You cannot complete your application online. You must appear in person. You can do this at your local Social Security office. Make an appointment (as detailed in Chapter 1), and a representative will fill out the form with you. You must bring income and resource documentation including copies of your paycheck, bank statements, insurance policies, and the like. You will also need to show the mortgage on your house or your lease if you rent.

All changes in housing and income must be reported as they may affect your eligibility. If a family member moves in with you, it must be reported. If you rent a room in your house, the income must be reported. If you move to another location, you must let SSI know. Your payment amount depends on your income, your resources, where you live, and other factors. Any change in your circumstances may change your eligibility or the amount of your award.

Your wages and other income must be reported to SSI monthly. You can do that in person or online—and I'm happy to report there's an app for that. So, you can send your report in from your Smartphone.

The amounts listed on the <u>Federal SSI site</u> for 2014 are $721 per month as the maximum payment for an individual and $1,082 as the maximum payment for a couple. If you are not collecting Social Security and are relying solely on wages, the benefit may be higher. Your state may also provide additional benefits if you qualify.

All but four states—Arizona, North Dakota, West Virginia, and Mississippi—offer a supplement to low-income seniors.

The federal Social Security Administration is paid by eleven states and the District of Columbia to administer their program. Those states are: California, Delaware, Hawaii, Iowa, Montana, Nevada, New Jersey, New York, Pennsylvania, Rhode Island, and Vermont. If you live in one of these states and apply for SSI benefits, you will apply through Federal Social Security for both federal and state awards. Should you qualify for both, you will receive one payment that includes both benefit amounts. This does make it easy. Should you live in one of the other 35 states, you will need to apply separately with your state to receive their SSI benefits.

It is worth applying to your state because if you are collecting Federal SSI and are covered under Medicare your state may pay your Medicare premiums. You may also be entitled to prescription drug benefits, food stamps, and other government programs. This is public assistance and you will be required to provide documentation regarding your assets, income, and your housing arrangements.

If you are entitled to this benefit, it means you are living at or near poverty level and can get the help you need to insure you have the basic necessities of food, clothing, and shelter. I know some people will be uncomfortable with this option, but if you are unable to generate any additional income and you qualify for these benefits, you need them. They are essential for your existence. Take them. This program was designed to help you in a difficult time, and you should take any assistance available to you. Do not suffer pointlessly. Do not delay in applying for benefits, it could lessen your benefit and may decrease your chances of being eligible.

Chapter 4

Retirement Plans

"Money, it's a gas
Grab that cash with both hands and make a stash"
—Pink Floyd

The basic retirement plans in the U.S. are the 401(k), the pension, IRA, and Roth IRA. Each type has different variations depending on the company you work for, the company you invest with, and who manages the plan. We will discuss the basics of each plan, how they are funded and how the distributions (payments) work.

401(k)

The 401(k), named for the Internal Revenue Code that authorized it, is a defined contribution plan adopted by the IRS in 1978. It is a voluntary plan whereby employees can have a certain percentage of their salaries automatically deducted and placed into an investment account. Many companies offer to match a certain maximum percentage—often 4 to 6 percent, though sometimes more, sometimes less.

It is optional for an employee to participate in a 401(k) plan. If offered, you can choose to opt in or opt out at any time. You also choose what percentage of your salary you want to contribute. These 401(k) accounts are individually owned by each participating employee. The employee is responsible for choosing how the funds are invested.

Companies are not required to offer a 401(k) program or match a specified amount or percentage. They offer this program as a benefit to make working at their organization more attractive. Should you leave your job, the funds go with you. This made it much easier to move from job to job than with a pension, which is a <u>defined benefit plan</u>.

In a defined *contribution* (401(k) plan, the amount you contribute is specified, but the amount you are paid out is *not* guaranteed. It is determined by the company match and the performance of the investments you make.

In a defined *benefit* (pension) plan, the amount you are paid (the benefit) is a specified amount determined by your salary and years of service.

The funds for your 401(k) come out of your salary before it is taxed (pretax dollars). You do not pay income tax on the money before it is invested. The funds are invested as you direct so that you may generate earnings on your money. The holdings can be withdrawn at any time, but unless certain circumstances apply, you will incur a penalty if you withdraw before age 59½. At age 59½ you can withdraw any amount without penalty, but you do have to pay any tax due on the money.

You do not have to begin payments at age 59½, but you must begin withdrawals by age 70½. This is called the Minimum Distribution. The amount of funds you must withdraw is determined by a formula based on how much you have in your account and your life expectancy. If you don't take funds out at this time, you will be heavily fined.

Now that we know the basics of the 401(k), or 4-0-wonk, as Phoebe on Friends calls it, let's see how our benefits are paid out.

Once you reach age 59½, you can start drawing on your 401(k) fund without penalties. You can begin this process anytime between 59½ or 70½. After 70½, you are required to take a minimum amount yearly. You can take 100 percent of the amount out at any time during that age range, but you will have to pay federal, state and local tax on it all when it is withdrawn.

You can set up monthly or quarterly payments for a designated amount and a designated period of time. You would then pay tax on just the amount that is withdrawn at a specific time. You can also choose to take yearly allotments. Most likely your income at this time will be less than before and so your taxes will generally be lower.

There are many calculators online to help you see what you can expect from your 401(k) payment options. The site mycalculators.com provides one. You can enter how much you currently have invested, how much longer you plan to work, and how much time you want your payments spread over. You can choose a 10-year plan, a 20-year plan, or another. Most programs allow you to change your distribution choice yearly, so it is not permanent once you set it up.

Your payments can be configured to fit your needs at any time, as long as you have enough funds in the account. If you want to start collecting at 59½ to boost your income and improve your lifestyle, you can. If you want to hold onto it to ensure you have more when you are older, you can do that too. You can take it out and spend it or spread it out over many years and have a steady income stream. That's your personal choice. You need to remember that these funds are not for life like Social Security. When the money runs out, the checks stop coming. So plan carefully.

If you are still working and eligible to participate in a 401(k), start participating now. Contribute enough to get the free money the company match provides. In the end when you do retire, you will have accumulated your contribution, your company's match, and any gains you make on the investment. Having something is better than having nothing.

Every little bit will matter when you retire and are not receiving a steady paycheck.

I know many financial planners who recommend that if you are over 50 to put the maximum amount allowed into your 401(k) each year until you retire. For most of us, this amount will be much too high. The maximum is currently $17,500 and an extra $5,500 as a catch-up provision that allows those 50 and over to put an extra $5,500 a year into their account to try to "catch up" and increase their retirement savings. Between the two amounts, that comes to $23,000 you can contribute per year. That amount is definitely not an option for most people. It's certainly not for me.

One of the features of 401(k) plans is that you can withdraw funds from your account at any time, but if you do so before turning 59½ you will incur a 10 percent penalty.

According to expertplan.com, you may withdraw funds without a 10 percent penalty under these conditions:

1. "If you become totally disabled.
2. If you are in debt for medical expenses that exceed 7.5 percent of your adjusted gross income.
3. If you are required by court order to give the money to a divorced spouse, a child, or a dependent.
4. If you are separated from service (through layoff, termination, quitting, or taking early retirement) in the year you turn 55 or later."

In all of the above situations, you must still pay the federal, state, and local tax due.

Some plans allow you take loans against your 401(k) under approved conditions. In this case you can avoid penalties and taxes. Repayment of the loan and the interest owed will be deducted directly from your paycheck.

Many plans have different policies. Check with your Human Resources Department or your plan manager to see what your specific plan regulations are.

Once you retire or leave an employer, you may be able to leave the funds in your 401(k) account, but you may need to roll them over to an IRA. This depends on your specific plan. There are no tax consequences because you are moving from one tax-deferred account to another. Timing is very important though. If the funds are not deposited in the new account by the due date, penalties and taxes will apply. Contact a tax or investment professional in these circumstances to make sure the transition goes smoothly.

One aspect of the 401(k) is that when you die, funds in your account can be passed on to a beneficiary. But, the amount will be considered income and subject to federal, state, and local taxes. The money may also be considered part of your estate and might be subject to estate tax as well.

A *Designation of Beneficiary* form stipulates how you want the funds in your retirement account dispersed upon your death. It is important to keep this form up-to-date as it takes precedence over a will. Any time there are changes in your plan, you change jobs, or management companies, you need to update your form to ensure your wishes are carried out. You can get these forms from your plan administrator. Give copies to your beneficiaries, executor, or lawyer.

If you wish to leave your funds to your children, and your form is deemed invalid, the funds will automatically go to your spouse, even if you've only been married a short time. The spouse is not obligated to carry out your wishes and may elect to keep the money.

If your will and valid Designation of Beneficiary form do not designate the same beneficiaries, the form wins over the will in a legal battle. To change who gets the money in your retirement plan, you must change the form.

The 403(b) is similar to a 401(k) but is available only to certain groups such as teachers, non-profits, cooperative hospitals, and self-employed ministers. There are specific requirements for employers to be able to offer a 403(b) plan.

Pensions

Pensions are funds that pay a designated amount to an employee upon retirement, usually for life. There are many kinds of pensions and ways of funding them. If you have a pension you will need to check with your plan manager for the specific details of your plan.

Any employer may provide a pension plan for its employees, but it is now more typical of government agencies, unions, and insurance companies. It is often considered a deferred compensation—work now, get paid later, plan.

The amount of your benefit is calculated by a set formula based on your salary and number of years of employment.

Employees, generally, have lifetime benefits. Whether you live to be 60, 80, or 100, you will get the same monthly benefit with periodic cost of living adjustments.

Pension benefits cannot be passed down to a beneficiary. Unlike a 401(k), the assets are not in individual employee accounts, but a general fund. The money is not considered yours until you receive it. Once you pass on, the payments stop. However, some plans do have survivor and disability provisions.

Pensions are not optional and can be funded in different ways. In some only the employers make contributions. In others, both the employer and employee contribute. There are also some that are unfunded, where the benefits are paid directly by the employer and not from a pooled fund.

Most non-government pension plans are insured by Pension Benefit Guaranty Corporation. Should your company file for bankruptcy, you can still be paid your monthly amount. Federal pensions fall under the protection of OPM.

There has been great controversy over the value of the 401(k) as compared to the pension. Many financial experts see the 401(k) as the cause of the retirement financial crisis we are experiencing today.

According to Edward Siedle, a contributor for Forbes, "Americans also know the great 401(k) experiment of the past 30 years has been a disaster. It is now apparent that 401(k)s will not provide the retirement security promised to workers. As a former mutual fund legal counsel, when I recall some of the outrageous sales materials the industry came up with to peddle funds to workers, particularly in the 1980's, it's almost laughable—if the results weren't so tragic."

Here are the basic benefits and drawbacks of the 401(k) and the pension.

In Summary: 401(k) vs. Pension
Benefits of 401(k)
1. Purchased with pretax dollars
2. Tax on investment gains are not paid until withdrawal
3. Your gains can be reinvested and continue to earn
4. Employers may match part of your contribution
5. It is easier to change jobs
6. You decide how your money is invested
7. You can borrow against it
8. Upon your death, the balance of your account goes to your estate

Drawbacks of 401(k)
1. Not a guaranteed monthly income

40

2. Benefits end when your money runs out, not when you die
3. Responsibility of saving is on the employee and you can opt out leaving yourself with no retirement plan
4. Many do not know how to manage their investments properly
5. Vulnerable to fluctuations in stock market
6. Often has high and and/or hidden management fees
7. Not insured

Benefits of Pensions
1. Guaranteed automatic payments for life based on a formula of salary and years of service. Pensions insured
2. Employers must contribute
3. Large fund can withstand fluctuations in the market
4. Low management fees
5. Managed by professionals for greater returns
6. Because funds are pooled can take greater risks near retirement age

Drawbacks of Pensions
1. More difficult to change jobs
2. Benefit does *not* increase when stock market does
3. Benefits stop when you die. They are not passed on to your estate
4. No control over how money is invested
5. Government agencies or company susceptible to bankruptcy

As the state of the finances of current retirees shows, 401(k) accounts have not provided adequate income for retirement. Pensions, on the other hand, have a long standing record, are less risky, and provide income for the lifetime of the retiree.

It may be too late for current retirees to benefit from this knowledge. But it's not too late for the next generation. They need to demand better retirement programs or face the same problems we have now.

Pensions in general have a solid record over a long period of time. They are low-risk, provide income for the lifetime of the retiree, and are generally worth more than a than a defined contribution plan.

Individual Retirement Account (IRA)

A traditional Individual Retirement Account is purchased by an individual and not through an employer. Anyone can open an IRA account as long as they have received taxable earnings during the year and are not over the age of 70½.

The maximum yearly contribution to an IRA for someone over 50 is $6,500. Like a 401(k) the IRA is acquired with pretax dollars, but as you probably noticed the maximum contribution is much lower.

The 401(k) allows someone over 50 to contribute $23,000, where the IRA maximum is $6,500.

You must have earned income to purchase an IRA, and you can only contribute as much as you have earned. You can, however, contribute the full amount of $6,500 for a spouse from your earnings.

Similar to a 401(k), you can begin distributions at age 59½, and there are certain circumstances where you can withdraw funds before then without penalty.

1. First-time home purchase
2. Education expenses
3. Death or disability
4. Medical expenses that won't be reimbursed
5. Health insurance—if you are unemployed

You do have to take minimum distributions at age 70½ or face stiff penalties.

Remember that you must pay the taxes on the amount withdrawn at the time of disbursement. Don't be fooled into thinking you have more money in an IRA than you do. You must consider the taxes. You have to think of all of these things when figuring out your retirement income.

Traditional IRA accounts can be converted to a Roth IRA (below), but Roth IRAs cannot be converted to traditional IRAs. You may want to choose a low-income time in your life to convert from one to the other, thereby decreasing the tax bite. Then when you retire, all of the funds in the Roth account will be tax-free. If you have a Traditional IRA and a Roth IRA your contributions together cannot be more than $6,500.

SEP IRA is an IRA for people who are self-employed. With this, a self-employed individual can contribute up to 25 percent of their income. The maximum contribution is $52,000 per year.

Roth IRA

What makes the Roth IRA different from most other plans is that its contributions are made with after-tax dollars. This means that you pay the tax on the contributions before buying the plan. When you withdraw the funds later, you do not have to pay tax on your original investment or on your earnings. When you get a payment from a Roth IRA, it is all yours, free and clear, and does not count as taxable income.

A Roth IRA may not be the best suggestion for people close to retirement. They are considered good for younger workers who plan on being in a higher tax bracket later in life. The dividends earned on investments will be compounded over a long period of time, and will never be taxed. You pay taxes on your contributions at the time they are deposited, but you never pay tax on the earnings.

Like a traditional IRA, the contributions for a Roth IRA must come from earnings, and the maximum amount you can contribute for those over 50 is $6,500. The Roth IRA has income restrictions which may decrease the amount you can invest.

Unlike a 401(k) or traditional IRA, you must hold the funds for at least five years from your first contribution, even if you are 59½ years old. If your account began five years before turning 59½, you can begin getting payments then, if not you will have to wait past that age.

There are no mandatory withdrawals at 70½. You never have to take a penny out. This makes the Roth IRA a good way to leave a tax-free inheritance if you have built it up over time. The heirs, however, are required to take mandatory distributions over their lifetime.

Now we know how the benefits of the most common retirement plans are distributed. With the 401(k) and IRA, we can begin withdrawing funds at age 59½ without penalty. We must pay tax on any monies taken out, and it is mandatory that we begin taking payments at age 70½. It is also important that we know that these are *not* lifetime benefits: when the money runs out, the checks stop coming.

Roth IRA withdrawals are tax-free, and no mandatory distribution is required.

If you do have a retirement plan, whichever it is and no matter how much it is, it will help make your financial future more comfortable and more manageable.

Chapter 5

The Big One

"So bye, bye Miss American Pie"
—Don McLean

"I'm coming Elizabeth. It's the Big One."

It was pretty funny when Fred Sanford stumbled around his living room clutching his chest, but it's not so much fun when it's happening to you. Believe it or not, this chapter is the Big One—the one that will have the most impact on your finances, your lifestyle, on the quality of your life, and ultimately your happiness in retirement. It's your health and it's big indeed.

I know we've all heard it over and over again, if you have your health....

Right now that's truer than it ever will be. Being healthy decreases your doctor visits, it decreases the number of medical tests you need, it decreases hospital visits, *and* it decreases the number of prescription you take. Good health adds up to a big plus on your bank balance and determines how you are going to spend the rest of your life.

According to beforeitsnews.com, in 2013, 60 percent of U.S. bankruptcies were due to medical bills. 78% of those bankruptcies *had* health insurance.

It's no secret that improving your health has incredible rewards, but it often seems a very daunting, confusing task. It doesn't have to be. It may be easier than you think. Losing weight is the one factor that will have the most impact on your health.

Most of us have tried to lose weight at some point in our lives. We may have been unsuccessful, or been successful temporarily, and then gained the weight back. We have a goal to look good for a reunion, a daughter's wedding or another event—and then when the event is over, we go back to the same old eating habits and gain the weight back.

In our mind, once we have reached the goal, we're finished. We can check that off the list. The task is done.

Our goal above was to lose a certain number of pounds in a certain time frame. Think for a minute if we were to change the goal. Instead of just losing weight, let's change the goal to being healthy in retirement.

If you want to be healthy, attaining and maintaining a healthy weight would support that goal, not *be* the goal. This is an important distinction because the goal to be healthy is ongoing and won't stop when you reach a certain weight. Instead of the on-again, off-again diet mentality, the focus is on long-term health, not an event or another temporary goal. The focus is on *you*.

There are many programs out there, and you may find a structured program works best for you, particularly if you have a lot of weight to lose. But, it is important to know that small changes can amount to big results as far as your health goes.

My friend, Michael, lost his brother to heart disease at a very early age. His brother, Rex, was obese and required a septuple bypass heart surgery. It caused Michael to take a hard look at himself and his own health. He was 55, overweight, and pre-diabetic. His two favorite foods were ice cream and French fries, and he ate these pretty much every day.

For starters, he gave up eating just those two things. He was surprised by the difference the change made. Within a year he was no longer pre-diabetic. What are the two foods you eat the most that are adversely affecting your health? Stop eating them and see what happens.

Now, you can't give up French fries and replace them with onion rings or anything else. You need to take them out of your diet completely.

According to Dr. Kathleen Zelman of WebMD, "A little goes a long way when it comes to weight loss. Research has shown that losing 10 percent of your body weight—or less—can have big payoffs for your health. Such a small loss may not seem like much if you're trying to look svelte in your jeans. But in terms of your health, it can be a big victory."

There are many simple things you can do to improve your health and lose weight without making it overwhelming. One is to change your plate size. Start eating your meals on a nine-inch salad plate. That alone is going to decrease your food intake. One reason many of us are overweight is that we eat too much. We no longer know how much is enough.

To take it one step further, divide your nine-inch plate into quarters. One quarter is for protein (meat, chicken, fish, eggs), another quarter is for carbohydrates (pasta, rice, potatoes, bread) and the last two quarters are for vegetables. This is a simple way of getting accustomed to appropriate portion sizes. This alone will help you eat the right foods and the right amounts of those foods.

Another straightforward method of eating well is to buy foods only from the *perimeter* of the store. The aisles around the outside have all of the *fresh* foods: meat, fish, produce, dairy. The aisles in the center of the store have all of the *processed* foods that are definitely not the best choices for a healthy diet.

Beverages can be a big source of calories and an easy way to lose weight. A 20-ounce sugared beverage (soda, iced tea, energy drink, juice) has approximately 250 calories. A

Big Gulp has 500 calories. If you switched one 20-ounce sugary drink a day to a glass of water or a zero-calorie beverage—and if you kept everything else exactly the same—you would lose over 26 pounds in a year. Give up one Big Gulp a day, and you would lose 52 pounds in a year. Add some small changes to your diet and that weight will start melting off.

Consider 250 calories times 365 days per year is 91,250 calories. Divide that by 3,500 calories per pound, and you come up with a weight loss of 26 lbs.

We've just talked about four easy ways to change your health:

1. Stop eating two foods you eat often that are not good for you.

2. Eat your meals on a nine-inch plate divided into quarters.

3. Eat only foods from the perimeter aisles of the supermarket.

4. Give up sugary beverages.

Choosing any one of these will get you started on a healthier road today. Which one will you choose?

My own story is a little different. My parents owned a candy store and soda fountain while I was growing up. Ice cream sundaes, chocolate egg creams, licorice whips, and Mary Jane's sound like every kid's dream, but it turned into a lifelong love of all things sweet and creamy and a lifelong struggle with attaining—and maintaining—a healthy weight.

When I talk about structured programs, there are countless products available and I have tried many. Weight Watchers, NutriSystem, and Jenny Craig are the most popular and can be effective. Unfortunately, for many participants, the focus is on short-term weight loss. I was successful on all three of these programs, but did gain the weight back after I had reached my goal. I know how very frustrating it is to work so hard, succeed—and then end up exactly where you started or worse.

A few years ago, I found a program that worked for me and focused on a healthy weight as part of a long term health plan. I lost 30 pounds and have been able to maintain that over time. I am not perfect, by any means, but have managed to achieve a good overall balance in my health and eating habits. I got so much out of the program, that now I help others reach their goals too. I do my coaching over the phone or via the Internet. I'm always happy to help others reach their health goals. It's very rewarding and it keeps health in the forefront of my mind on a daily basis. Please send an email to me at retirementbasicsforboomers@gmail.com for more information.

While individual health is crucial, the health of our nation is in urgent need of attention, too. Our country is suffering from an epidemic. We are caught in a web of ever-increasing poor health and ever-mounting medical costs. In the next chapter we will view health from a national perspective.

Chapter 6

It's Bigger than You

"Doctor, my eyes have seen the years and the slow parade of fears
without crying
Now I want to understand"
—Jackson Browne

Being overweight or obese is a major cause of preventable health problems in this country. I know it is a very personal issue and can be uncomfortable to talk about, but I think the stakes are too high to ignore it.

First of all, understand that being overweight is not your fault. It's not your lack of will power, or lack of control. There are many factors making you eat more. You are sabotaged by temptation day and night.

We are all humans, and the primitive part of our brain knows nothing except how to instinctively survive. It is this brain that seduces us into eating more and more food. The mechanism behind this is so that in times of plenty you eat as much as you can. You eat all that is available and store up fat. That way when food is scarce you have reserves to carry you through the tough times. We feast in times of plenty to survive the times of famine.

The problem is we live in the land of plenty. Most of us *never* go hungry. We keep storing up energy, but the famine never comes and we get bigger and bigger and bigger.

That being said, even though it is not your fault, *you* are the one who suffers the consequences and, therefore, only you can fight the circumstances stacked against you.

The second factor is *what* we eat. Our food is laced with addictive substances to make it taste better and to make you eat more. There are added sugars, salt, and fat to enhance the flavor, but also to get you hooked. There are many studies that show that <u>sugar is as addictive as cocaine.</u>

We live in a capitalist society. Food companies are in business to make money. Adding addictive substances and making food more palatable increases their bottom line, but at what cost? How much control should the government have in the ingredients that go into our food?

There is a case in New York City where The Board of Health is trying to limit the size of sugary drinks as a way to fight obesity. People and especially the soft drink industry are up in arms to fight this law. Michael Grynbaum of *The New York Times* states that this law is more important than limiting soda. It sets the precedent for "how far local governments can go to protect the health of their citizens."

Now we get to advertising. Have you ever been sitting on the couch watching TV and a commercial comes on for pizza? You see that pizza coming out of the oven with the melted cheese and the crispy crust. The next thing you know, you're up at the refrigerator peeking in to see what you might have that will satisfy your craving. You may have just eaten, but for some reason, all of a sudden you want more.

Often just the suggestion of a food can make us salivate. Trust me, food companies know this. Millions of dollars a year are spent researching and developing what to expose you to, so as to get you to eat more and more. Guess what? It's working.

You're on your way home from work, and you pass a fast food restaurant that is sending the scent of grilling burgers wafting through the air. On the spur of the moment, you find yourself on line at the drive thru. They've sucked you in.

"I can't believe I ate the whole thing!" Remember that? Drug advertising has added to the problem. Eat too much, take a pill. The pill is responsible for making us feel better. We are no longer obligated to make wise choices and stop eating when we've had enough. This may work in the short-term, but in the long-term, you are the one who is suffering. So, "Plop plop fizz fizz" on outta here and start choosing for yourself.

As you can see, you are bombarded at every turn with carefully planned food additives and advertising campaigns to manipulate you into eating large quantities of food and then a drug to make you feel better afterwards. You are continuously poisoned and brainwashed. While the food and drug companies increase their profits, you are the one suffering with metabolic syndrome and going broke from paying the outrageous medical bills associated with it.

I'm not done yet. The portion sizes in restaurants have grown exponentially to ridiculous sizes. According to the December 2010 edition, *Gastroenterology & Hepatology*, an independent peer-reviewed journal, since its opening in 1955, an order of McDonald's fries has grown by 250 percent, a soda by 475 percent, and a hamburger by 500 percent.

"Where's the beef?" That was an award winning commercial saying "our burger is bigger and therefore it's better." Where's the beef now? Unfortunately, it's around our waistlines.

When Starbucks opened it offered two sizes, 8-ounce short and 12-ounce tall. Now we have 16-ounce, 20-ounce and the 31-ounce Trenta. While that is a lot of coffee, it is also a lot of calories. Unsweetened Trenta drinks can be about 230 calories. Sweetened drinks like the Iced Peppermint White Chocolate Mocha can be more than 600 calories.

Give up one 600-calorie Trenta drink per day and lose 62.5 pounds a year.

Other sugary drinks are also a major cause of weight gain and its associated illnesses. Intake of sugared sodas, teas, energy drinks, and fruit juices has increased dramatically over the last 30 years. There is no doubt that this increase has had a significant contribution to the obesity epidemic and subsequent disease, according to the definitive Framingham Heart Study.

Remember, give up one 20-ounce sugared beverage a day and lose 26 pounds in a year. Give up one Big Gulp a day and lose 52 pounds in one year.

Getting healthy is not just for appearances sake. There are many medical conditions associated with being overweight and inactive. These include but are not limited to heart disease, diabetes II, high cholesterol, high blood pressure, liver disease, depression, and cancer. Weight problems also cause joint stress causing pain in the feet, ankles, knees, hips, and back—often requiring surgery. Excess weight also contributes to difficulty walking and breathing.

Fatty liver disease is on the rise, and we are faced with a growing epidemic. It occurs in about 10 percent of children and 20 percent of adults. There are currently no drugs to treat this disease and the only way to reverse it is with changes in diet and exercise. Without these changes, a liver transplant may be necessary in order for you to survive.

According to Dr. Ronald Busuttil, chief of the division of liver transplantation at the David Geffen School of Medicine at UCLA, 6,000-7,000 liver transplants are performed in the U.S. every year and there is a waiting list. Doctors estimate that by 2025, of the 25 million people who will then have fatty liver disease, 5 million will need transplants. The transplant system will be overrun. Where will we ever get that many livers?

This disease can be reversed with simple changes in diet and exercise, yet drug companies are racing to create a drug that will treat it. This is the absurdity of our culture. One industry spends millions to get you to eat more of something that makes you sick, while another industry is spending millions to find a cure.

Let's see: you could lose a few pounds or lose a liver and possibly your life. Is that a tough decision?

Having obesity related diseases like fatty liver disease, diabetes II, cardiovascular disease, high blood pressure, and cancer cause you great financial strain, and they also can severely decrease the quality of your life. As you come into retirement age, you want to be able to do the things you like to do, whether they be fishing, walking, biking, playing with your grandkids, swimming, traveling—or all of the above. Many of these activities can be difficult when you are overweight. Depression is common in overweight individuals who often feel helpless against the conflicts they face. The emotional toll and lack of self-confidence can be devastating.

My friend's mom visited Colorado last summer. She was so embarrassed because she had to buy two seats on the plane to come out here. Another woman was told she couldn't ride the rides at Disney because she was too large. This was really humiliating. Retirement can be a great time in your life. Don't let being overweight rob you of wonderful experiences. Take charge of your health.

Overweight? You have a lot of company.

The CDC says that 66 percent of Americans are overweight or obese. The population of the U.S. is about 300 million people. That 66 percent means that 200 million people in the U.S. are overweight. I've been one of them, but think about how many people that is and how much suffering is associated with it. Think of what the medical bills amount to. The cost is staggering.

Recent estimates claim that obesity alone adds $190 billion in medical costs. The total estimate for increased medical costs for obese and overweight care is $450 billion. This is just medical care. Other associated costs are high absenteeism, higher workers compensation cases, decreased productivity, and higher fuel costs in transportation. We are bankrupting and weakening our nation.

What do we do? Being overweight or obese is the most common cause of preventable illness in the U.S. next to smoking. Public education and subsequent laws banning smoking over the last 30-40 years have been very effective in significantly decreasing smoking and its associated diseases.

While many public awareness programs are being put into effect regarding obesity and its health effects, it may be several years, if not decades, before their full results will be felt. In the meantime, we need to take matters into our own hands and exercise our rights to choose.

Government policies may be hampered because the answers to the problem may be in direct conflict with some of the values the people of this country hold dear: capitalism and personal freedom. There is a lot of resistance to government controls as to what goes into our food. There is resistance to limiting food advertising and resistance to any regulations limiting the portion sizes and the amount of food any individual consumes. I think we need to get past the conundrum, and address what is most important: your health and your life.

There are an estimated 112,000 DEATHS PER YEAR attributed to obesity. Medical experts feel that this number is grossly under-reported as many deaths may be attributed to a specific disorder, such as heart failure, diabetes II, or cancer, and not necessarily as a part of the overall illness, obesity. The real death toll may be two or three times that.

112,000+ deaths per year, while all of these deaths are tragic, let's put that into perspective.

From 2001 until the present (13 years) there have been 6,717 American deaths in Afghanistan and Iraq combined.

In 2010 there were 40,393 drug-related deaths in the United States.

And there are 112,000 deaths per year from obesity.

We have a War on Terror.

We have a War on Drugs.

Why don't we have a War on Food?

What do you think the reaction in this country would be if a virus were killing 112,000+ people per year? Would we be this complacent?

Obesity kills an overwhelming amount of people. Millions of others are afflicted with debilitating diseases that cause untold pain and suffering for the individuals themselves and those that love them.

While our government goes bankrupt from health costs, what can you do? Vote with your dollars. The only thing that will make food companies change what goes into our food is a decrease in sales. If you stop buying it, they'll stop making it.

We may not have an immediate solution for the country as a whole, but we can change our own behavior and the foods we bring into our households. Small changes can amount to big results when many are making them.

You matter. Your choices matter. Get healthy. Save your retirement. Save your life. Bring down the cost of medical care and help decrease the national debt. Join the war on food. It's Patriotic.

Chapter 7

Activity

"My grandpa, he's 95
And he keeps on dancin' he's still alive
My grandma, she's 92
She loves to dance and sing some, too
I don't know but I've been told
If you keep on dancing you'll never grow old"
—Steve Miller Band

Of course, there is another important piece to the health puzzle and that is activity. We Americans are busy. We are stressed. The wrong foods sap our strength and energy. It can be hard to get started, and it is hard to move when you are overweight.

Remember, we are all starting at our own individual place. No two bodies are in the exact same condition. Take stock of where you are and do something appropriate. Take a walk. Take the dog. Take your spouse. Take your girlfriend. Walk alone, and enjoy the peace and quiet. Walk whenever you can.

If you cannot walk, do chair exercises. Lift your legs one at a time. Circle your ankles. Lift your arms, circle your wrists, roll your shoulders, and circle your head. Your body needs movement to function properly. Little by little you'll be able to do more and more.

If you have trouble getting started, take a class at a gym or health club. If you need guidance, you can get a DVD and workout at home. There are hundreds of programs online for all types and levels of exercise. The great thing about these is that you can do them at any time. You can fit them into *your* schedule. You can try different activities to see what you like and what will work best for you.

The point is move, do something. Keep at it. You'll be better for it.

Speaking of moving, when I first moved to Aspen, I was surprised by the activity level of everyone here. I would ask a friend what she was going to do for the day. She'd say: "Well, I took the dog for a hike, then I went to yoga and after that Pilates. This afternoon I'm going for a bike ride and then I'll stop by the Club, sit in the sun—then take a swim."

I went back to bed. I was exhausted just listening to her.

People here are extreme. My second winter, my friend Ci asked if I wanted to do the Aspen Uphill with her. Without giving it much thought, I said sure. I had hiked some over the summer and felt I was in good enough shape to hike up Aspen Mountain.

Not so, Kemosabe.

Uphill races, common here, start at 7 AM, so they don't interfere with the ski day. At that hour it can be pretty cold and this morning it was 7 degrees at the bottom of the mountain. One thing that's great about hiking in the summer is that the higher up you get, the cooler it becomes. This is also true in the winter, but not so great.

I trudged up the mountain, slowly. I was embarrassed to see people of all ages passing me—people in their 60s, 70s, 80s, and perhaps 90s. It was grueling for me, but it seemed like nothing to them. Well, I was the penultimate racer. I use that word hoping no one knows that it means "next to last." There was a guy behind me, and he was in his 30s. That helped a bit. They post the results in the local newspaper, and fortunately for me, they are kind enough to leave the stragglers out.

The point is that people here are active. I see people of all ages out hiking, biking, skiing, and doing just about every activity I can think of. They are healthy and vibrant. They are inspiring and engaged with their environment.

I may never attain the level of fitness that many locals here enjoy, but I have improved. Two years ago I did the Aspen Uphill again and had a respectable time of 1:31. It was in the paper. I was hoping to get under 1:30, but I think I was close enough.

The important thing was that I was better than before, and you can be too. No matter where you are in your life and no matter what your current activity level, you can get started. You can do a little more.

As we've discussed, eating well and exercising are the backbone of your goal of good health. Losing weight and getting fit could be the best and most rewarding things you have ever done for yourself. You don't have to be extreme— a little goes a long way here. Start today. Exercise and a healthy weight will certainly have the most impact on your individual health, your finances, and on how well you are able to live your life.

Chapter 8

Wills, Inheritance, and Living Wills

"When I die and they lay me to rest
gonna go to the place that's the best"
–Norman Greenbaum

One of the kindest and most thoughtful gifts you can give to your loved ones is to have your affairs in order before you leave this world. You might think there's no need, but it is always better if you designate how you want your funds and possessions dispersed. If you don't, you can leave a long legal process for your family and state law will determine the outcome.

Items with sentimental value can be left to specific individuals, but it would probably be easier and more meaningful, if you gave those things to your loved ones while you are still here or discussed them before you go. This can help dispel bad feelings and avoid family friction that could come from surprises in the will. You don't want to leave a family feud behind. Iron out as much as you can before you go. You'll feel better and so will those who love you.

You cannot completely disinherit a spouse, even if you want to, especially in community property states. It is considered that a spouse is a joint owner of some of your estate. You do not, however, have to leave anything to your children or any particular child. You cannot leave money to your pet. However, you can set up a trust and executor for your pet's future care. Leona Helmsley set up a $12 million trust for her lucky dog, Trouble.

In an effort to follow my own advice and leave instructions for *my* fortune, I created an unofficial trust to assure the care of my dog, Shanti. Yes, she is spoiled, and I want her to stay that way or at least spend the last years of her life in comfort.

I asked my sister, the beneficiary of my 401(k), if she would use those funds to make sure Shanti is taken care of. My friends in Colorado have agreed to care for her themselves, or find a good home for her in her later years. (Thanks guys.) My account will pay for her needs during that time. While it isn't as much as Leona left, it should be enough to keep Shanti in dog biscuits for as long as she wants them.

Wills

You can easily create your own will. If you have a simple estate, you can use a Last Will and Testament from the internet. You can fill it out online or by hand and have it signed by two witnesses. The witnesses should not be beneficiaries or anyone who has an interest in the outcome of the will.

You can handwrite a will and have it witnessed and therefore legal. A holographic will is one that is written, signed, and dated in the handwriting of the person making the will. Witnesses do not have to sign the will, but the handwriting needs to be verified by a disinterested party. Holographic wills are legal in about 25 states. Before writing one, check the current law in your state to verify it is legal.

One of the purposes of a will is to make your wishes clear. Make sure your statements are not ambiguous in any way and truly express what you want. Another purpose of the will is to establish that you are making these communications with a sound mind and without undue influence. Express your wishes in a clear, concise, manner leaving no doubt about your intentions or your state of mind.

Remember that a *Designation of Beneficiary* trumps a will. Make sure you do not have conflicting instructions and always check to insure that your designation form is up-to-date and valid.

If your situation is complicated in any way, have a lawyer draw up the will or at least review a will that you have created yourself. Once you have created a will, you need to leave it where it can be found. It is not recommended to have it in a safe, safety deposit box, or other location with limited access. You may want to send a copy to the executor, leave a copy with your lawyer, or have one with your insurance policies or other important papers. It does you no good if nobody can find it.

Wills and finances are also emotional matters. Many families have difficulty talking about death, and money is taboo, too. A will is your final communication to those you love and the world you leave behind. Make it a good one.

Inheritance

The flip side of the will is inheritance. It can be a wonderful thing, and it is very nice that a loved one wants to share with you and take care of you when they are gone. But it can be a double-edged sword and can bring a lot of mixed emotions: you generally lose someone you care about at the same time as receiving an inheritance.

Inheritance can be a great gift that can lighten your financial burden and make positive changes in your life. As we discussed before, money and death are two things that are awkward to talk about in this society. If you are the giver, talk to the recipients of your gift so that they can prepare.

There may be estate tax or inheritance tax. Being aware and prepared can be very beneficial.

Inheritance is *not* a good retirement plan. Things change. People can get married, divorced, have fights—anything can happen. People are living much longer now and may outlive their finances. If long-term or nursing home care is needed, the expected giver may deplete their funds before they pass on. The point is inheritance is never a sure thing until the money is actually in your bank account. Don't count on it. Consider it a nice bonus should you be fortunate to receive one.

Any monies or property you inherit may be subject to an estate tax, inheritance tax or both. The estate tax is based on the value of the deceased person's estate and subject to tax according to the state the giver resided in. An inheritance tax is based on who receives the property, their relation to the deceased and where they live.

Only a few states charge an inheritance tax. They are Iowa, Kentucky, Maryland, Nebraska, New Jersey and Pennsylvania. Nineteen states have an estate tax. New Jersey and Maryland have both. My sister is unlucky to have homes in both of those states. She would definitely have to pay the max. Where the deceased lived and where you live will determine the tax due on the estate. For each state there are certain amounts that are exempt. Here are the exemptions for each state.

There is also a federal estate tax. However, the estate must be worth more than $5,340,000 for the tax to apply in 2014. Not something most of us are going to have to worry about.

Inheritance can be a blessing and change your life. Having things in order before the time comes can save an enormous amount of red tape, time, taxes, and hard feelings. Make the best of it, if you are one of the lucky ones.

Living Wills

As people are living longer and medicine has advanced, individuals and their families are faced with a new problem. When is the appropriate time to let go? What measures do you want taken and in what circumstances do you want to yield to the inevitable? Making these decisions can be a heart-wrenching experience for your loved ones, and if you make that determination before the situation occurs, you can give your family great peace of mind. The decision is yours, not theirs.

With a living will, you can leave instructions as to what life-sustaining procedures will be administered or withdrawn and when. There are many situations you might not want to live through, especially if the outcome doesn't change. Other individuals feel they want every measure taken to ensure they live as long as they possibly can. This is a very personal choice that represents your values. You have a right to make your own health care decisions, which includes your right to refuse treatment.

Living Will or Advanced Health Care Directive laws vary by state. This website leads you to a list of states and the forms accepted by each. You may also want to sign a Medical Durable Power of Attorney designating an agent to make medical decisions for you if you are no longer able to do so yourself. Make sure your forms are state-specific and give copies to your agent, your doctor, and hospital.

Any of us could face a serious medical crisis at any time. There is no reason *not* to be prepared and have the comfort of knowing that your wishes will be honored, and you can live your last days with dignity.

This book is not intended as a substitute for appropriate legal counsel. The reader should consult with an attorney or other professional for all legal matters. For accurate personal guidance in all matters included herein, the services of a qualified professional should be sought.

Chapter 9

Living in the USA

"Get your motor runnin' Head out on the highway
Lookin' for adventure and whatever comes our way"
—Steppenwolf

Retirement brings major changes and for many people it means a change in location. Many dream of moving away from snow and ice to a warmer, sunnier climate. Now that you've got the time and are not tied down to a job, you may consider moving. The next decision you'll have to make is where to go?

Now that you've figured out what your income will be, it's easier to determine what locations will work for you. You can narrow down your options by spending some time answering a few questions.

What is important to you?

Is it essential to be near family and friends or are you ready to put some distance between you and them?

Do you like four seasons or would a year-round warm weather location suit you just fine?

Do you have a sport or hobby you'd like to pursue?

Do you like art, music, and culture—or more rustic living?

These are some of the basics that can help you figure out a place you will be happy. It makes no sense to move if you are *not* going to be happy.

Consider your weekly routine. Where do you spend your free time? Is religion important to you? Is there a place of worship you are comfortable with in your new location? Church is a great way to meet new people and become part of a new community.

University towns can be very inexpensive. There is often less expensive housing and an abundance of activities. Students bring life and vitality to a place, and that may be just what you need. Many seniors enjoy taking classes and learning new skills.

As we all know, health is an important issue when considering a new location. Do you have particular medical issues and need access to certain services?

Spend some time. Think it through with your spouse, partner, or friend. Discuss this in detail so you both understand your objectives and agree to a place. It's not going to be fun for anyone if either of you are dragged somewhere you don't want to go.

Understand too, that no place is perfect. You'll always have to make some compromise; just be sure you can live with your decision.

I am one of those unusual people who like to move. To me it is similar to doing a fast or a cleansing. I get rid of anything cluttering my life. It makes me feel free and unencumbered. (I guess I am a nomad at heart.) But it's worth mentioning here that you don't have to move. You may be perfectly content exactly where you are, and if your finances support your decision, that's great. Many folks do find that they don't want to continue with the upkeep and expense of a big house. Downsizing to a condo or apartment can free you from the headache and stress of maintenance and repairs. It may be a big load off your mind and relieve you of unwelcome responsibility. The whole point here is to make your life more enjoyable.

If you have decided to move, now you need to choose a location. Since we are all on a limited income, we'll start with a list of the least expensive cities in the U.S. to live in. These are cities: remember there may be even less expensive places to live in the surrounding areas.

10 Cheapest U.S. Cities to Live In

Kiplinger, June 2013: "10 Cheapest U.S. Cities To Live In"
This information comes directly from Kiplinger and shows the cities in the United States that have the lowest cost of living. This website changes on a regular basis. Click on it for the most up-to-date list of places. The information is based on data from The Council for Community and Economic Research. They take into account the cost of rent, food, utilities, transportation, health care, and other goods and services. These are cities with at least a population of 50,000.

Harlingen, Texas, is the least expensive city in the U.S. The cost of living is 18.4 percent below the national average. It has award-winning hospital facilities, a huge plus for many retirees. There are a host of retirement communities and senior centers.

Pueblo, Colorado at #2 boasts both a low cost of living and a dry climate. The cost of living is 16.6 percent lower than the national average. It has senior housing available through local government. If humidity is not for you, Pueblo might be the place.

Norman, Oklahoma's cost of living is 16.2 percent below the national average. Rents are low, residents report higher incomes, and there is a low rate of unemployment. This may be a good spot for those looking to work during their retirement. Norman is famously the home of the University of Oklahoma.

If you want to live in a big city, *Memphis, Tennessee*, has it all at bargain prices. At 14.6 percent below the national cost of living, Memphis is the least expensive major city in America. Its location on the Mississippi is perfect for its involvement in the shipping and transportation industries.

Idaho Falls, Idaho, is one of our cooler retirement locations. It has an incredible outdoor lifestyle. There are plenty of winter sports available in the cold, snowy weather with hiking, biking, rafting, and more in the summer. There's a high quality of life at a low cost of living (14.4 percent below the national average) and very low unemployment.

Youngstown, Ohio, is closer to Pittsburgh than Ohio's major cities. It has a cost of living 13.5 percent below the national average. With home values being 73 percent less than the national median, expenses are well below average.

In *Jonesboro, Arkansas,* costs of everything from groceries to utilities to health care are low. Dental and optometrist visits are 27 percent lower than elsewhere in the U.S. At 13.3 percent below the national cost of living, you don't need a lot of income to live here.

Wichita Falls, Texas, comes in 13.2 percent below the average cost of living. The top employer in the area is Sheppard Air Force Base. Incomes are solid, and the unemployment rate is low.

Temple, Texas, is an hour north of Austin in Central Texas. The overall cost of living is 12.9 percent below the national average. There is a strong economy and a low unemployment rate.

Augusta, Georgia, also has a cost of living of 12.9 percent below the national average. Aside from the week of the golf Masters, Augusta is affordable. Housing costs are low at 26.5 percent below average. Groceries and other household expenses are well below the average as well.

This list should give you some of the basic information for these places and some things to ponder. Consider if one of these might be right for you.

For me it was interesting to read about Idaho Falls. It has a lot of the same qualities as Aspen, without the big price tag. Idaho Falls has a population of 57,000. Aspen's is about 7,000. I may not want to live in the city proper, but a smaller town outside of it might be just what I'm looking for.

If you have your choices narrowed down, find out as much as you can about each place. Research, ask questions, discover the good neighborhoods, or more importantly, the bad. Plan a site visit. The more prepared you are, the more you will get out of your visit.

I find too that when you talk to people and tell them you are thinking of moving there, you get a wealth of information. People are generally more than happy to share their opinions. Visit. Stop to socialize for information you may not get from websites and guidebooks. The locals can help you get in the know about the town. Often there are things available that you may not be aware of until you have been there for a time, such as employee housing in Aspen. This insight can help you save before you even get there. You might make some friends, too.

There are other affordable places that are rated on livability. If you do have a small retirement plan or some savings, these may be the right choice for you. They are

LIVING IN THE USA

touted as the most affordable, livable cities for retirees by several sources. There are many places here worth considering:

1. *Spokane, Washington.* It has moderate temperatures and all four seasons. It has less than half the rainfall of Seattle making it a very attractive location in the Pacific Northwest. There is a strong focus on culture, parks, and recreation.

2. *Pittsburgh, Pennsylvania.* Touted as a city that has turned itself around. Pittsburgh was voted most livable city for several years by many top-notch publications. Its small size and friendly neighborhoods offer a comfortable lifestyle. The University of Pittsburgh and other colleges offer a wide range of classes and activities.

3. *Des Moines, Iowa,* has been named the "best city for business" in the U.S. Des Moines has a low cost of living and lots of opportunities for retirees. Your money will go further here. Des Moines was named America's wealthiest city by *USA TODAY.*

4. *Fort Myers, Florida,* boasts a high percentage of retirees and retirement complexes. Golf and tennis are high priorities. Housing prices have been low since the economic downturn. Florida has no state income tax, making it even more attractive.

5. *San Antonio, Texas.* Caters to a substantial retiree population. It is located near the center of Texas and is famous for its River Walk. It is a large city with a large tourist base that might make getting a part-time job easy.

As you can see there is no shortage of low-cost domestic retirement opportunities. Choosing the right one for you and your income, will take some exploration on your part.

There are many opportunities and places with a low cost of living for retirees in this country. You can pick the option that is best for you not only budget-wise, but also a place where you can have a life you can enjoy.

Even though you are moving within the United States, each place will have its own unique customs and way of life. Moving from New York City to Aspen, for example, required a big adjustment and I was not prepared for it.

New York has just about everything you could want, any time you want it. There is shopping everywhere. In Aspen, the closest department store is four hours away in Denver. I always wondered why people would spend their vacations in New York shopping, when there were so many other great things to do—now I know.

The entertainment in NY is never-ending. Aspen has one movie theater, and if you miss a movie, you might miss it for good.

Food delivery was the most difficult to live without. This is a New York amenity that once you are used to is *soooo* hard to live without. You can get any kind of food delivered to your home whenever you want it. There's Chinese, Thai, Italian, Indian, Sushi, anything you can think of. The food is good and in general very reasonable. My favorite was Sunday morning breakfast delivered from the coffee shop. You could have a great big breakfast, and the only effort you had to make was to answer the door.

I have to admit that Aspen did have things that New York did not. There was the skiing and the breathtaking bluebird sky. Then there was the "Elk in Heat Urine" sold in Wal-Mart. (I kid you not. Hunters apparently use it. I don't even want to think about what for.) Then there was the fact that every morning on the news they announced which bugs had hatched overnight. At first I thought they were desperate, really desperate, for news of any kind, but I later found out that this is vital information for those who spend hours standing in the water trying to lure a fish onto their hooks just to throw them back. In New York, you get to sit in a boat, drink beer, and actually eat the fish you catch. Go figure.

My point is things are going to be different: Some *good* different and some that take some getting used to. It's best if you embrace your move as an adventure and enjoy the diversity. The beginning is the hardest time, as you are confronted with things you may not have thought about, but you can adapt. I no longer miss New York. I enjoy it as a visitor and love the variety and excitement of life there. But I appreciate my active, quiet, life now, though I do eat a lot of frozen meals.

State Taxes

Now that we've explored some attractive locations, we can look at tax implications for some states. Taxes can be a factor in considering where to live. A high tax rate can really eat into your income, and that is something we are trying to avoid. There are seven states that do not have an income tax:

1. Alaska

2. Florida

3. Nevada

4. South Dakota

5. Texas

6. Washington

7. Wyoming

Tennessee and New Hampshire only have tax on dividends and interest income. As you can see, some of the states with cities with a low cost of living also do not have a state income tax. This makes those states even more attractive for those on a limited budget.

As with all financial matters taxes are personalized, and you need to ask a tax professional what are the best choices for you in that regard. There are many factors to consider, and a professional opinion will help you choose best.

Moving can be fun, and it can be stressful. Change can be difficult if you let it be. Do your research, visit, know as much as you can, and then expect the unexpected. The more prepared you are, the better you will handle it and the more exciting it will be.

Chapter 10

Living Abroad

"Aruba, Jamaica, ooh I wanna take ya
Bermuda, Bahama, come on pretty mama"
–The Beach Boys

In conversations about retirement, moving overseas is always a hot topic. The ocean is always bluer on the other side of the equator. We all know or have heard of the wonderful places, the low cost of living, and the incredible experience of moving to an exotic land. Trust me, I can think of nothing better right now, as I endure spring in the Rockies. But, I would like to know what the reality of making an international move is like. What does it take? Do you just show up? Is it as easy and as great as it seems?

In this chapter we will look at a handful of those locations and get a realistic look at what you need to do to live there or become a legal resident. What kind of lifestyle would you like to have? There are the sunny, sandy beach communities, towns in the mountains, big city life. Which is for you? I've lived in all three of those types of environments, and it makes the choice more difficult. Each has its advantages, and you will have to decide which is best for you at this time of life. For me it's challenging, because I like them all.

For some a warm tropical climate, walks on the beach with palm trees, and the smell of salt air is their dream spot. For others a mountain location with a cooler climate and less humidity may be right. You might like the fast pace and the hustle of a big city with all the conveniences that come with it. You don't have to give up your dream of having those things. It's all out there. You just have to find the right locale for you and your budget.

There are several countries that welcome retirees and do their best to make coming to their shores attractive and inexpensive. Both Panama and Ecuador have incredible discounts for retirees. They want you. They want American dollars to boost their economy, and they make it easy for the retiree to get long-term or permanent visas.

The discussion below is not intended to be exhaustive by any means, but just a brief overview of the most popular retirement destinations.

Remember, countries are large and individual places within a country will be very different. Think about someone moving to the United States. What would you tell them it was like? Like the beaches in California, the intensity of New York, or the slow southern tempo of Kentucky? Explore online, in books, in social media. Get on the expat websites and blogs. Make your research an adventure. Find the place that is most appealing to you. Then go visit.

The expatriate or expat community—people who live outside their native country—are a great source of firsthand information. Numerous websites are available for nearly every location that attracts retirees. There are many well-established expat communities throughout the world, and it's nice to have a contact or two when you arrive at your new destination.

Visa Requirements

For each country you may consider relocating to, there are basic visa requirements that you must provide. You will need:

Visa application
Visa fee
Passport photos
Current Passport-good for six months
Health certificate
Criminal background check

All documents will have to be validated by a government agency and notarized. There may be additional legal or translation fees required to process your application.

Financial Requirements

Each country will then have its own financial requirements. The most popular locations with a low cost of living are listed below. I will caution you that information on the Internet can be incorrect and outdated. It is best to get your information directly from the embassy or consulate for the country you choose. Requirements change frequently as does the process involved. I have also seen websites mimicking official sites with offers to process your paperwork for a fee. Look carefully and make sure you are on an actual government site. Most end in .org.

Panama, in Central America, is currently the #1 country in the world for attracting retirees, with a generous discount program for *pensionados* and a modest income requirement. You must prove an income of $500 per month for an individual or $600 per couple from a government or corporate source for a long term visa. There is no deposit required to live in Panama. While the length of the visa is indefinite, you do need to prove annually that you have the necessary income to remain in the country. The Turista Pensionado is the best option for those collecting Social

Security or a pension. Contact the embassy for the most up-to-date information info@embassyofpanama.org.

Discounts are available for just about everything: transportation, entertainment, restaurants, utilities, hospital visits, medical and dental care as well as prescriptions. They range between 15 and 50 percent for retirees and make living here much less expensive.

Ecuador, a South American country, is also a popular retirement destination. It boasts an attractive discount program similar to those offered in Panama. One additional feature is that retirees never have to wait in line. You automatically go to the front. We New Yorkers like this. Waiting in line is our least favorite pastime.

For immigration purposes for Ecuador you must apply for the Pension Visa and prove an income of at least $800 per month. There is no deposit necessary.

Mexico, our nearest neighbor to the south, has long been a retirement destination for many Americans. To immigrate, you must first apply for a Temporary Resident Visa. The Temporary Resident Visa lasts up to four years. According to the Consulate, you must prove $2,000 tax-free income per month or an average balance of bank accounts and investments of $95,892 over the past 12 months. After the four-year period, you can then apply for a Permanent Resident Visa. For this you need an income of $2,500 per month or a balance of $119,865 for the past 12 months.

Belize is a small country on the Caribbean just south of Mexico. The Qualified Retired Persons Visa (QRP) is a long-term visa available to those who can prove an income of $2,000 or more per month.

Nicaragua, a Central American country, which has both a Pacific and Caribbean Coast, requires an income of just $600 per month and is working hard to compete in the arena for the attention of retirees.
info@ConsuladoDeNicaragua.com.

The Philippines is a South Pacific country made up of over 7,000 islands with an SRRV or Special Resident Retiree Visa, the most appropriate for American retirees. This visa requires proof of $800 monthly income or $1,000 for a couple and does require a $10,000 deposit. If you do not have a verifiable income, you can still obtain this visa, but the deposit requirement goes up to $20,000.

Malaysia is a South Pacific nation that is connected to the mainland of Southeast Asia by Thailand. This is known as West Malaysia. Another section located on the northern side of the island of Borneo is called East Malaysia. The two are separated by the China Sea. Malaysia offers the MM2H, Malaysia My Second Home, visa. This is a ten-year renewable visa. A deposit of $45,878 is required along with a monthly income of $3,058 (at today's conversion rate).

Thailand in Southeast Asia has long been a popular retirement destination. It offers the Non-Immigrant Long Stay visa, which allows you to stay for one year. After that you must reapply, and an extension may be granted. A verifiable income of about $2,015 per month is required or a deposit of $24,800.

As we have seen, income requirements vary a great deal. Some are very low at $500 per month, and others are over $3,000 per month. Deposits can be high or not needed at all. For me, this limits my choices, which in a way, makes it easier. Your income and the type of environment you want to live in will help determine which place is right for you.

General Attributes

One of the things that all of these countries have in common is that they are in a warm climate—some warmer than others—but they are all closer to the equator than we are. It is also generally true that the cities will be more expensive, though the further away you get, the lower the cost of living. Also, the closer you are to the metropolitan centers, the better the services will be.

Most of these countries are continually upgrading their infrastructure to accommodate the growing number of immigrants—and yes, you will be an immigrant—but some are further along than others. As a general rule, medical care, utilities, water, Internet connections, and cell coverage will vary the farther away you get from the city. (I live in a rural area here in the U.S., on the Western Slope of Colorado, and there are many places where there is still no cell service.) The more remote the location, the less reliable the services. If you need the Internet or a cell phone to conduct business while abroad, you'd want to make sure you have what you need before making the move.

Road conditions are also something to consider: though they are improving all the time, the existence and maintenance of roads are a major factor. If you like to travel and explore, this may be something you want to think about and investigate.

You may also want to consider the distance you live from a good hospital and how long it will take for you to get there in an emergency. I currently live two-and-a half hours from a major hospital so that would not be new to me, but I know I can be airlifted out on fairly short notice in a crisis. If I needed to be driven, the roads are excellent, and it would be a smooth ride. It's not fun to imagine traveling on a bumpy road when you are sick or hurt.

Language can be a fun factor. In general, more English is spoken in the city than in the rural areas, unless you are in an area with a large expat community. It is always easier, and you will acclimate better if you speak at least a little of the local language. You'll be able to communicate with your neighbors and handle situations better. You'll be more engaged in your community and have better relationships. Another perk is that learning a language is one of the best things to do to keep your mind sharp, and we could all use *that*—so start creating those new pathways in the brain.

Shopping is another thought. Many cities cater to the expat communities and import things you are used to. Merchants want to keep you happy, so they import foods and products that you like. This may not be true in more rural areas. I'm not much of a shopper, but one thing I did notice is that people in other countries are generally much smaller than Americans. At 5'7" I felt like a giant in a clothing store. I couldn't fit into any of the clothes.

We all need to remember that we live in a highly efficient country. Things here work. That is not always the case elsewhere. Electricity, water, phone service, etc. may all be subject to outages or spotty service.

Administratively, there can be problems that seem so easy to fix. You will face dealing with what will seem like ridiculous and redundant procedures, and there may be nothing you can do about it.

Best to learn and endure. You are not going to change things and will be frustrated trying.

In many countries you cannot just walk into a bank and open an account. You need referrals and documentation from other banks and institutions. Not a big deal in our world, but it can be in theirs. This can be a Catch 22 because you can't always get a bank account without a residence, and you can't get your utilities turned on unless you have a bank account. Try to get an account open before you move or at least before you want to take a shower.

Worth noting: Your Social Security benefit can be directly deposited into your bank account in many foreign countries. If the country of your choice is not listed, check with the Social Security Office. It still may be possible. Cuba and North Korea are definite no-nos.

Health insurance is something you need to look into. Medicare does *not* cover you when you are outside the

United States, but Medigap might depending on your policy. You may be able to join a local healthcare plan, but some countries, like Malaysia, require you to carry your own policy. Because of the low cost of care, many expats choose to pay out of pocket when they need care and forego the regular cost of insurance.

There are numerous ways of calculating cost of living and plenty of conflicting information. Numbeo.com claims to have daily updates, and it is very simple to use. You can put in any two cities and do a comparison of the costs. They can be in the same country or different ones. You can compare cost of living in Bangkok to Phuket or Bangkok and Kuala Lumpur. You can also choose the currency you want the results in. You don't have to try and compare Malaysian Ringgits and the Thai Bhat and then try to figure out what that means to your budget in U.S. dollars.

Popular Places

Panama has the advantage of using the U.S. dollar as its currency. There is a great amount of American influence here because of our association with the Panama Canal, which is now being expanded. The major metropolitan center is *Panama City.* English is spoken widely, and the most prominent hospital is affiliated with Johns Hopkins.

Boquete is the most popular mountain town and is noted for its year round spring-like temperatures. The entire district has a population of only 25,000, and it is known for its large artist community. Nature lovers flock here, too. There are a multitude of outdoor activities, birding being among the biggest, because there are over 900 species in the region.

Coronado is nicknamed the "Hamptons of Panama" and is a popular beach community among expats and locals alike. It has a lively strip of restaurants, bars, and shops, but there are quieter and less expensive towns in the surrounding areas.

Ecuador also uses the U.S. dollar as its currency and that makes transactions much easier. No need to do conversions in your head all of the time. *Quito* is the capital, and its best feature is that it is 9,350 feet above sea level. This gives it a very pleasant climate and makes it popular with retirees. It has all the conveniences of a modern city and English is widely spoken.

Cuenca is in the southern mountains and also has a moderate climate. It has a population of over half a million but has a low cost of living and offers great value for your dollar.

Salinas is Ecuador's most popular coastal town and is a large tourist destination known for being one of the least expensive beach towns in the world. Keep in mind that you will not be catered to as an expat here. You'll have to live like the locals.

Mexico has so many places and options to offer. Though famous for its fabulous beach resorts, there's much more to Mexico. There are several large cities, as well as mountain towns and art centers.

Ajijic in the Lake Chapala region is in the mountains about 30 miles south of *Guadalajara*. It has a moderate year-round climate and an extremely large expat population.

San Miguel de Allende is a colonial city located in the high desert of Central Mexico. It has narrow cobblestone streets filled with local folk art and music. A favorite spot of Frida Kahlo, it is popular with both artists and retirees alike.

Mazatlan is on the Pacific Coast north of Guadalajara and due east of the southern tip of the Baja peninsula. It offers a coastal community at more affordable prices than most other Mexican resort areas.

Belize uses American currency, and English is the official language. It offers many tax advantages, which makes it attractive to some from the U.S. Belize also boasts extraordinary beaches. Snorkeling and diving here are unparalleled and attract people from all over the world. For serious medical care you would want to fly to the U.S. or Mexico, though the country is working on improving both its infrastructure and hospitals.

Nicaragua is a relative newcomer to the retiree scene and is also working to improve its infrastructure. The most modern medical facilities will be found in *Managua*, the capital, but the two largest expat communities of *Granada* and *Leon* offer quality care. Both are colonial cities and offer a large cultural experience.

The Philippines was once a Spanish Colony and is a predominantly Catholic country. Your Spanish may be helpful here as many words are incorporated into the local language. The capital is *Manila*, which offers a modern lifestyle with a variety of entertainment, shopping malls and advanced medical facilities.

Cebu is the second largest city and is considered a charming major metropolis. Cebu is a long island with access to wonderful beaches and world-class snorkeling and diving. Many feel that Cebu is the best place for American retirees in the country.

Baguio is in the mountains and is known as the "Summer Capital" because of its cooler climate. It is the center of higher education with many schools and students in the area. Outside the city proper you'll find gated communities and lower rents. Baguio is also the major retail area of the region and local and imported goods can be bought at cut-rate prices.

Malaysia has invested in providing world-class medical care at reasonable prices and therefore attracts people from all over the world. Its doctors have been trained at the best medical schools, and hospitals have invested in state of the art equipment. Infrastructure is excellent, and expats are catered to in the big cities.

Kuala Lumpur is a melting pot of cultures and offers the finest in shopping and in varied cuisine.

Penang is an island off the west coast and is famous for its beaches, parks and gardens. English is widely spoken, and there is a large expat community. Yet, the cost of living is much less than Kuala Lumpur.

I mention *Kuching*, mostly because I think it's a cool place, on the northern side of the island of Borneo—remote and quite exotic. There are over 30 ethnic groups and many languages are spoken. There is a small expat community, cost of living is low, and best of all for me, there are many trips available into the forest, which has unique plants and animals not seen anywhere else in the world. Further south on Borneo in Indonesia, an orangutan orphanage and rehab center await deep in the jungle. You'll be happy to know that headhunting is now illegal.

Thailand is famous for its low cost of living, tropical climate and high quality medical care. *Bangkok* has excellent infrastructure and a great public transportation system. It is multicultural and a regional business and financial center. It has also been voted the "World's Best City" four times by Travel and Leisure.

Phuket is Thailand's famous beach attraction with white sandy beaches and aquamarine waters. It is given to warm, sunny breezes and a laid-back, tourist atmosphere. Over 20 percent of the permanent population is expats. I guess they like it here.

Chiang Mai is in the northern mountains and has a cooler climate. Rents are cheap, and food is a real bargain. It has all the modern conveniences yet is surrounded by a multitude of Buddhist temples. Many find Chiang Mai charming and appealing.

Should You Move?

So you see there's a big wide world out there, at all prices, just waiting for you. There's adventure and fun to be had, if that's what interests you. You have to ponder a few questions and determine what you want your life to be like.

Are you adventurous?

Do you like cultural diversity?

Do you make friends easily and fit right in or prefer a quieter life?

Do you need quick access to the U.S.?

You need to consider if you have special health needs, require constant Internet access, and where your money will buy you the most.

It's all out there. All you need to do is pack up and go!

Chapter 11

Savings Ideas

*"She works hard for the money
So hard for it, honey."*
—Donna Summer

My friend, Amory Lovins, energy physicist extraordinaire, coined the term *Negawatt*. He means that before we create more energy, we need to stop wasting what we have. Otherwise, we will lose much of what is newly created.

The same principle applies to savings or what I call *Negabucks*. The best way to have more money is to cut down on spending. We need to plug the holes in our budgets and stop letting our money get away from us.

Housing is your biggest expense. Finding an inexpensive place to live or finding others to share the expenses could afford you a lifestyle you could never have on your own. Having a social life and support system, whether it is family or friends, is one of the most important keys to living a longer and happier life.

The Golden Girls got it right. They figured it out. They found others in similar situations. None of them had enough money for retirement, but together they had it all. By sharing a house and expenses, they could afford a lifestyle they could never have had on their own.

They also became friends, really more like family. They developed a support system and they took care of one another. They didn't worry about being alone and how they would manage if they were ill or incapacitated. They were confident they were loved and important to others in their lives. I think we can take a lesson here.

Sophia Petrillo, the most golden of the girls, might say: "Saving money is not rocket science. Just spend less than you earn, you yutz!" And she'd be right, but somehow it doesn't always work out that way. Try as we might.

If we work at it, there are many ways to save money. We may be doing some of them now, but cutting a few more corners might make us a lot more comfortable. Make saving a game. Challenge yourself. Keep track. Know that what you are doing is making a difference. Don't look at it as depriving yourself. Think of it as financing your future. Congratulate yourself when you've saved a certain amount. Celebrate when you reach a goal.

We all know to give up our afternoon Starbucks and bring our own lunch to work. The next big saver is cable and/or satellite TV. Either cut it out altogether or cut your premium channels. You can get many shows on Hulu, Amazon, Netflix, or others for free or a much lower fee. With wireless or a simple cable, you can get them right on your TV.

Another advantage to getting rid of your cable is you don't have to watch commercials. This can be one of the biggest hidden money savers of them all. If you are not watching commercials, you don't know what products you are missing. You don't "want" for things you shouldn't have, and that makes you happier. You are not tempted by delicious-looking food and you eat less. TV is generally boring: as we watch we have a tendency to also eat.

Watching less may lead to a big improvement to your health. And, if you are not watching TV, you are doing something else. Maybe an activity, visiting with friends, volunteering: whatever you do, it is more stimulating and will help you enjoy life more and fight off depression.

Watching a lot of TV can have devastating results for a lonely aging person.

TV commercials are not the only culprits. Catalogs, email ads, magazines, and newspapers are nearly as detrimental. Advertising of all kinds affects us adversely. Most Americans get catalogs in the mail on a regular basis. Any catalog you order from is going to send you an email nearly every day showing you what's on sale, what the new products are, and offering free shipping.

These are all ploys to separate you from your money and most times for things you can do without. If you haven't seen the new line at Macy's, it's not in your consciousness: you don't know what you are missing, and you don't feel deprived. If you need something by all means shop for it, but don't be lured into believing you need things when you don't. Throw away all of your catalogs. Don't even bring them into the house. Delete all junk emails. Do not read them. Don't fall victim to magazine and newspaper ads and don't get roped in by sales. Shop for what you need, when you need it.

Next time you go shopping, put everything you bought on the table and examine it carefully. Separate it into items you truly needed and items you wanted but could do without; those you buy out of habit; and impulse purchases. Get the calculator out, go over the receipts and see how much less you might have spent had you shopped more wisely.

When I did this, I found that at least half of the items I bought were unnecessary. I had bottled water, Diet Coke, dog treats (my dog would insist these are essential), and many other items I could certainly live without.

Day cream, night cream, eye cream, hand cream, body lotion, lip balm, face wash, body wash, bath soap, hand soap, dish soap, dishwasher soap, and laundry soap. I'm not even that clean.

Fact is most Americans buy much more than they need. We Boomers are conspicuous consumers. Most of us have too much stuff.

Just look around you. Look in your garage, in your attic, in your cabinets and your closets. We are enveloped in a world of needless things. The good news about that is we have so much room for improvement. We can learn the difference between essential and extraneous items. It's not that hard. Below are some suggestions to save money right away in your everyday life. There are many other ways and many lists online with hundreds of suggestions. Have a look and see what ones might work for you.

Cleaning—I looked in my cabinets. I had toilet bowl cleaner, Scrubbing Bubbles, Mister Clean, Windex, disinfectant wipes, Carpet Fresh, Febreeze—might some of these be combined? You think I watched commercials in the past? How else would I even know about these things?

My first suggestion comes from my friend Michele. Last winter she began making her own cleaning products from essential oils. The cost is so much less that the savings are enormous. A surprise benefit for her is that she didn't get sick all winter. Usually, she suffers from several colds and has a chronic sinus infection, so for her it was really noticeable. She saved money, avoided harsh chemicals, and adopted a healthier way of life.

My grandmother used to wash the windows with a vinegar solution and newspaper. She said it was the best way to avoid streaks. My mother cleaned the toilet with bleach. My friend Helen still cleans everything with Comet. (Josephine the Plumber must have made a big impression on her.) Using ordinary household items as cleaning products or one product for many functions is a great way to save money.

Another way to save on cleaning products is to buy concentrates. Companies like Melaleuca sell organic concentrates that save you money, keep you away from caustic chemicals, and do great things for the environment. Shaklee and Seventh Generation are other companies offering concentrated nontoxic products.

There are many ways of saving money, and you can find the ones that are right for you. Below are some other suggestions for decreasing your cost of living.

Shopping Tips—Create a budget, know what you can spend—and don't go over. Buy generic brands: most times they are just as good. Buy things made in the U.S., many are much cheaper now. Write a list and stick to it. Join rewards programs and check for coupons for those items before you go. Don't shop because you are bored. Compare pricing at different stores and Supermarkets. You may be surprised at the differences you find.

Remove your credit card numbers from internet shopping accounts. Get rid of the *purchase with one click* option: having to enter the number each time gives you the opportunity to rethink your purchase. Believe it or not, this has saved me a lot of money.

Use the library. Cancel magazines subscriptions. Borrow books. You don't need a Kindle to get electronic books. Amazon has a free Kindle app for your computer and phone. I use this all the time.

My brilliant friend Peggy worked at a department store during the Christmas rush. That way she got discounts on gifts and expensive winter clothes. She also had a job lined up year after year.

Home—Use programmable thermostats. Turn off lights. Change your light bulbs to CFLs or LEDs: they last longer and are more energy efficient. Use power strips which cut electricity to electronics not in use.

Put on a sweater rather than turn up the heat. Wear socks and use extra blankets to keep warm. Keep curtains closed during the day to keep the house cool in summer. Keep air conditioning set higher to save on electricity.

Lower your water heater temperature and turn off water when brushing teeth. You can save over 3,000 gallons per year and help the environment while you're at it.

Financial Savings—Don't pay maintenance fees for any banking you do. Call your credit card companies and see if you can get your interest rates reduced. Always ask for any fees to be waived, even if it was your fault. It can't hurt, and they often say yes. Pay your bills online and save on checks and stamps.

Clothes—Clean out your closet. We all wear the same items over and over even though we have many more things. Bring out the stuff hidden in the back. Just a few items will perk up a wardrobe.

A model friend taught me this. Always buy things in the same color scheme, so you can mix and match. It makes your wardrobe look much bigger with fewer items. This also saves a lot on shoes and purses and makes traveling easier.

Return items that don't fit or don't go with anything else you have. If you let them sit around, it's just a waste of money.

Car—Don't speed, keep your car well-maintained, and check the air pressure in your tires. All of these will increase your gas mileage and decrease repairs. Walk or bike. You save gas and improve your fitness.

Compare insurance rates before you renew. Prices vary considerably. Avoid paying the installment rate if at all possible.

Do you really need a car?

Health—Wash your hands with soap throughout the day. This helps avoid cold and flu and thereby doctor visits and medication. You'll feel better too.

Eat healthy foods in healthy amounts. Eating less means spending less. Eating well and exercising cuts down on medicals bills and prescription drug costs.

Take care of your teeth. Regular brushing, flossing, and dental cleanings save money in the long run. Let's keep that gorgeous smile.

Socialize with family and friends. Talk can dial down your worries and lift your spirits. You will feel better and perhaps decrease the need for therapy or antidepressants commonly used in the over-60 crowd.

Don't smoke, drink only occasionally. These are high-cost items with no real return and serious health risks.

Entertainment—Learn to say no to dinners out, movies, and travel some of the time. Suggest pot luck dinners instead of restaurants. This will also get you invited out more as others reciprocate. Tell friends and family about your desire to save money. This can be helpful with their expectations for going out and receiving gifts. Try to find free events in the community for you to attend together. Work at this. It can be well worth your while and keep you included in things while managing your budget.

Many restaurants offer two for one or buy one, get one free options. (Doesn't that mean the same thing?) Others have specials at certain times of day or on prix fixe menus. In Aspen there are local specials, for the people who are *not* on vacation. Take advantage of these opportunities and get out once in a while.

Does your town have a discount movie theater? You can wait until the hype for a movie dies down, and see it when it is offered at the lower price.

Rent a movie and watch it with friends. This brings the cost per person way down. Sign up for Netflix or another streaming service. You'll have unlimited access to movies at a low monthly rate.

Women--We pay more for everything. That's just the way it is, but there are things we can cut down on, or do ourselves, to help our financial constraints. Some you may not be able to live with, some you may not be able to live without, but there are definitely possibilities for savings here. Choose what works for you.

Do you buy the $20-$30 shampoo at the salon even though the $3 variety at the drug store will suffice? Do you color your own hair for $9? Or pay others to do it for you? (I used to pay $200 every six weeks in New York. Doing it myself saved more than $1,400 per year.) Do you have your nails done? Or can you do them yourself? Facials, Botox, $85 moisturizer, waxing, pedicures, massage—there is a huge potential for savings here, if you indulge in any of these. I gave most of these up long ago. Review your services; see what you can do without.

Be smart, be clever, be inventive. Small changes can amount to big things over time. You will be surprised just how much you can cut out of your daily budget. You will be more surprised at how little you will miss those things. The answer to all financial troubles is to spend less than we bring in.

Saving money will be one of the greatest assets and boosts to your budget during retirement. There are many things we do without thinking that can make—or more than likely—break us. Knowing what they are and making wise choices can increase our retirement dollars substantially in the long run.

We've addressed cutting our spending, so now let's take a look at increasing our earnings. Once you are free of the daily work commitment, a whole new world of opportunity opens up.

Chapter 12

Working in Retirement

"Now that ain't workin' that's the way you do it.
You play the guitar on the MTV."
—Dire Straits

Never underestimate the "Power of New." There is nothing as stimulating and exciting as newness. Remember moving to a new place or starting a new job? How do you feel when you wear new clothes? Pretty good no? You name it, if it's new; it's in.

As retirees, we can have *everything* new. It's all fun and different. It's not the same old monotonous job you've been going to for years. This time *you* get to choose, this time *you* get to dream, this time *you* can have what you want. This time you don't have the pressure of supporting a family, having to prove yourself, having to get ahead.

It's all about doing what makes you happy.

In a second career, what would you like to be doing?

So start thinking about it. Is there anything you've always wanted to try? If you've had the pressure of working for yourself, getting a part-time job might seem like a vacation. If you've always wanted to work for yourself and didn't have the luxury of trying, maybe now is the time.

There are many small businesses you can start without a big investment. Some don't take anything at all—writing, for example. You can freelance; you can copy edit. Write marketing materials for local businesses. You can start a blog. You can write a book. Once I did decide that I was going to write this book, it didn't seem like work. It was something I wanted to do. I didn't know if I would have the discipline or wherewithal to get it done, but I found myself getting up in the middle of the night to write just because I had an idea or a thought. Though I'm pleased with myself for actually doing it, it was the process that was most rewarding. I was involved, engaged, *alive*.

Try something, if it doesn't suit you, try something else. When ideas pop into your head, don't ignore them, explore them. They may take you somewhere you never thought you'd go.

Evaluate your skills. The computer enthusiast will always have clients, especially in our generation. Many of us often need help setting up new equipment, repairing old equipment, uploading software, and just getting the darn things to do what you want them to. Can you sense my frustration just thinking about it? Many of our generation have a slow learning curve and need help figuring things out on the computer, myself included.

Perhaps web design, Facebook pages, social media marketing. There's a wide open field out there. You could be a consultant for small companies, individuals, or local businesses. Put in as much time as you want or need. Put your talents and skills to work for you.

If you speak another language, tutor students or travelers. Do you play an instrument? Give lessons. Do you knit or sew really well? Teach at a shop or give a class at the local college, adult education, or senior center. Get busy.

If you like to tinker, paint, or garden, sell your services. Are you good with cars? Do minor repairs. No one likes having to take their car in and get their oil changed. Wouldn't it be great if someone came to your house and did it right in your driveway for less than you would pay at the service station?

Trade services with neighbors. Save them time and money. (I'll dog sit for you if you mow my lawn.) Be active, be involved, and be social. It's all good for you. Not having to pay for something is the same as earning more. Exchanging services helps everyone involved.

Cities are nothing more than small neighborhoods lumped together. They're not the cold, hard, lonely places they are portrayed to be. I lived in Manhattan for a long time. I knew the tenants in my building, the neighbors on my block, and the people in the surrounding area. Living in a city does not mean isolation. These are great places to network because the people are concentrated in a small area. City people are short on time and are willing to pay for services. Let them know what you can do for them.

Look for a niche. What are your strengths? What do you like to do? How can you earn money from it? If you are a good cook and like it, cater. Cook for parties for your neighbors or local businesses. Start a healthy meal delivery service. Young professionals love this. They want to eat well, but don't want to spend the time and energy cooking, and they're willing to pay. If you have one dish that people rave about, sell it. Many home businesses have started by baking a batch of cookies or fancy cupcakes.

If you are outgoing and have a large network of family and friends, there are a multitude of home businesses for you. You can do jewelry shows, Pampered Chef parties, makeup, vitamins, skin care, or clothing lines. There's money to be made here, and you can work as much or as little as you choose.

Having a business keeps you stimulated. As I mentioned, I help people lose weight and get healthy. It's a wonderful business because with the large rate of obesity, there are so many clients who need this service. Helping people is also rewarding. It does your heart good to be part of a person's effort to make life-altering changes. If you are good with people, all you need is a computer and a phone. Contact me at retirementbasicsforboomers@gmail.com for information. See? It's that easy.

As our population ages the need for healthcare workers is opening up. There's a great opportunity for unlicensed health workers such as home health aides, personal health aides, personal assistants, drivers. Some clients need help with daily activities, paying bills, and getting to appointments. Others are looking for companionship. If you self-promote, you do not need to work for an agency. You can take on two or three clients and work only for them. You also earn more that way.

Do you make crafts or gifts for your friends and family? Do people really admire them? You can sell any of your home made products on etsy.com. Many home businesses have grown to huge successes on this site in the last few years.

You can sell on Ebay, be a personal shopper, or even a move manager. Most people hate to move and can't organize well enough to move efficiently. Some people, me being one of them, like it and are good at it.

In one of my many jobs, it was my responsibility to remove all of the items in hotels or condos that were being remodeled. Sounds easy enough, right? Try emptying 86 hotel rooms and disposing of all of the items in three days. It does take some coordination. I worked with excellent movers, and we donated all of the furniture to Habitat for Humanity. Habitat sells the items to raise money to build homes for low-income families. On some projects they've made more than $250,000. Win-win-win.

Move Manager: it's something I'd never considered a marketable skill, but here it is listed on RetiredBrains.com. RetiredBrains is "the largest independent job and information resource for boomers, retirees and people planning their retirement." There's a wealth of information here so check it out.

There are many reasons to work during retirement. Some do it for pleasure. Others to keep themselves interested, involved, and stimulated. It's good for the mind and body. Others work because they need to supplement their income. Whatever the reason remember there are a host of opportunities available to you.

What talents or hidden skills do you have? What lifelong dream can you fulfill? This is the time to make them work for you.

This is not only for domestic locations, but international as well. While many countries don't permit retirees to work, there are many that encourage new businesses. Go to a location and see what they don't have. It's easy for us to notice because there are things we are used to that just may not be available. Perhaps open a clothing store with American sizes for your American friends.

I read an article about the increase in pet ownership in Mexico. People are having fewer children and now treating their pets like family, just like their American neighbors. As a pet owner I see the market for toys, clothes, beds, leashes, and collars. In Aspen we have doggie spas. I have been to a doggie birthday party. People shell out big bucks for this stuff and in many places in Mexico this could be a big hit.

If you love dogs, start a dog walking or dog sitting business. I pay someone $50 a day to stay with my dog when I am away. That's $350 a week. That's a low rate here and one reason I don't travel much anymore. Babysitters in Aspen make $20 per hour with $5 more an hour per additional child. Look for work in upscale neighborhoods where you can get paid more.

Start a concierge business—run errands, buy groceries, arrange parties, etc.

See if something strikes a chord within you.

We're retiring from one stage of life to another. It's a transition, not an end. This time we're older and yes wiser. We know ourselves better.

We know our likes and dislikes. We know if we want to be an accountant or not. We've *lived* it. We have solid facts and experience with how the world works. We can take this information and use it to build our new lives. This time the focus is on being fulfilled. What can you do that inspires you? If you're jumping out of bed in the middle of the night to get to work, you are doing something right.

Conclusion

"May your hands always be busy
May your feet always be swift
May you have a strong foundation
When the winds of changes shift
May your heart always be joyful
May your song always be sung
May you stay forever young"
—Bob Dylan

When I began my research for this book, I knew nothing about retirement. I didn't know how much I would get from Social Security. I didn't know what Medicare did or did not cover or when my 401(k) payments would begin. The whole process was unknown and intimidating. Retirement as a whole was a cloud of mystery.

Have I figured it out? Not entirely, but I have collected solid information to use to make decisions as my future unfolds.

Will I retire early? I'm not sure. But I do know the consequences if I do.

Will I move to another place in the U.S.? It's likely. The cost of living in Aspen is high, and the winters are cold and long. Perhaps I can find a beautiful mountain town in a warmer climate without the expense of a resort.

Would I consider living abroad? Absolutely! I can imagine the adventure and excitement of discovery in a whole new world. Borneo seemed so exotic and intriguing. I love the idea of trekking through the forests and seeing the unique plants and wildlife. But the financial requirements for Malaysia may be too expensive for me. Panama or Ecuador would be a more likely choice. They both have warm, mountain towns.

Will I work? Yes, because I need to supplement my income and also because I think it is important to stay motivated and engaged. I see it as an opportunity to be creative and explore new ideas on my own terms.

When I decided to share my research about retirement, I had you in mind. Someone who, like me was fearful and perhaps unaware of what to expect. I hoped to share what I learned so that you could have the confidence to move forward and plan a brighter, more comfortable future.

Thank you for reading this book. I hope this information is as helpful to you, as it has been for me and that with it you can make positive changes that will help you live a vital, more fulfilling life.

WebLinks

Chapter 1
Full Retirement Age
http://www.ssa.gov/retire2/retirechart.htm
Social Security Retirement Planner
http://www.ssa.gov/planners/
ssa.gov
http://www.ssa.gov/
Benefit Estimator
http://www.socialsecurity.gov/retire2/estimator.htm
Longevity Estimator
http://www.socialsecurity.gov/retire2/estimator.htm
Windfall Elimination Provision
http://www.socialsecurity.gov/pubs/EN-05-10045.pdf
Government Pension Offset
http://www.socialsecurity.gov/retire2/gpo.htm
Spousal Benefits
http://www.socialsecurity.gov/retire2/applying6.htm
Same-Sex Couples
http://www.socialsecurity.gov/people/same-sexcouples/
Survivor Benefits
www.socialsecurity.gov/pubs/EN-05-10084.pdf
Online Office Locator
https://secure.ssa.gov/ICON/main.jsp#officeResults

Chapter 2
Medicare
http://medicare.gov/
Medicare and You 2015
http://www.medicare.gov/Pubs/pdf/10050.pdf
Part A
http://www.medicare.gov/what-medicare-covers/part-a/what-part-a-covers.html
Part B
http://www.medicare.gov/what-medicare-covers/part-b/what-medicare-part-b-covers.html

Part C
http://www.medicare.gov/sign-up-change-plans/medicare-health-plans/medicare-advantage-plans/medicare-advantage-plans.html
Medigap
http://www.medicare.gov/supplement-other-insurance/medigap/whats-medigap.html
Companies approved by Medicare
http://www.medicare.gov/find-a-plan/questions/medigap-home.aspx
Part D
http://www.medicare.gov/part-d/
Medicare Plan Finder
http://www.medicare.gov/sign-up-change-plans/get-drug-coverage/get-drug-coverage.html
Extra Help
http://www.ssa.gov/medicare/prescriptionhelp/
Medicare Savings Plan
http://www.ssa.gov/medicare/prescriptionhelp/

Chapter 3
Supplemental Security Income
http://www.ssa.gov/ssi/
Federal SSI Site
http://www.ssa.gov/ssi/

Chapter 4
Defined Contribution Plan
http://en.wikipedia.org/wiki/Defined_contribution_plan
Defined Benefit Plan
http://en.wikipedia.org/wiki/Defined_benefit_pension_plan
401(k) Calculator
http://www.mycalculators.com/ca/retcalc1m.html

Chapter 6
Sugar is as addictive as cocaine
http://www.ncbi.nlm.nih.gov/pubmed/23719144
Metabolic Syndrome
http://en.wikipedia.org/wiki/Metabolic_syndrome

Medical Costs
http://www.phitamerica.org/News_Archive/10_Flaggergasting_Costs.htm
112,000 Deaths per year from obesity
http://www.cdc.gov/PDF/Frequently_Asked_Questions_About_Calculating_Obesity-Related_Risk.pdf
American Deaths in War on Terror
http://en.wikipedia.org/wiki/United_States_military_casualties_of_war
Drug-Related Deaths
http://www.cdc.gov/mmwr/preview/mmwrhtml/su6203a27.htm

Chapter 8
Last Will and Testament
http://www.8ws.org/last-will-and-testament-forms.htm
Exemptions on Inheritance Tax for each state
http://wills.about.com/od/stateestatetaxes/fl/2014-State-Death-Tax-Exemption-and-Top-Tax-Rate-Chart.htm
Advanced Health Care Directive
http://www.doyourownwill.com/living-will/states.html
Medical Durable Power of Attorney
http://med.wmich.edu/sites/default/files/Durable%20Power%20of%20Attorney%20for%20Healthcare.pdf

Chapter 9
10 Cheapest U.S. Cities to Live In
http://www.kiplinger.com/slideshow/real-estate/T006-S001-10-cheapest-u-s-cities-to-live-in/

Chapter 10
Turista Pensionado-Panama
http://www.embassyofpanama.org
Pension Visa-Ecuador
http://www.ecuador.org/nuevosite/Req_Visas_Inmigrante_e.php
Temporary Residence Visa-Mexico
http://consulmex.sre.gob.mx/washington/index.php/en/component/content/article/175

Permanent Resident Visa-Mexico
http://consulmex.sre.gob.mx/washington/index.php/en/compo
nent/content/article/171
Qualified Retired Persons Visa-Belize
http://www.embassyofbelize.org/consular-services/obtaining-
a-visa.html
Special Resident Retiree Visa-Philippines
http://www.pra.gov.ph/main/srrv_program?page=1
Malaysia My Second Home
http://www.mm2h.gov.my/index.php/en/
Non-Immigrant Long Stay Visa-Thailand
http://www.thaiconsulnewyork.com
Countries with Direct Deposit for Social Security
http://www.socialsecurity.gov/pubs/EN-05-10137.pdf
Cost of Living Calculator
http://www.numbeo.com/cost-of-living/comparison.jsp

Chapter 11
Golden Girls
http://en.wikipedia.org/wiki/The_Golden_Girls

Chapter 12
Etsy
https://www.etsy.com/
RetiredBrains
http://www.retiredbrains.com/

Song Credits

Don't Stop
Christine McVie

We Can Work It Out
Paul McCartney, John Lennon

ABC
The Corporation: Berry Gordy, Jr.,
Alphonzo Mizell, Freddie Perren, Deke Richards

You've Got a Friend
Carole King

Money
Kenneth Gamble, Leon Huff, Anthony Jackson,
Ronnie Moore, Charles Fearing

American Pie
Don McLean

Doctor My Eyes
Jackson Browne

Dance, Dance, Dance
Brenda Cooper, Jason Cooper, Steve Miller

Spirit in the Sky
Norm Greenbaum

Born to be Wild
Mars Bonfire

Kokomo
John Phillips, Scott McKenzie, Mike Love,
Terry Melcher

She Works Hard for the Money
Donna Summer, Michael Omartian

Money for Nothing
Mark Knopfler, Sting

Forever Young
Bob Dylan

Acknowledgements

My first acknowledgement must go to the Social Security Administration and Medicare. The extensive websites and online procedures are an enormous asset to us all. The staff has been helpful, polite, and knowledgeable. My experiences were all positive, and I commend them on a job well-done. In order as they unfolded. Thanks to:

Barry Berman, Executive Director, Infinity Culinary Training, whose simple act of kindness to a relative stranger started me on the road to writing this book. Also, I thank him for his *tinkering* with the text and improving it tremendously.

Adrienne Brodeur, Creative Director of the Aspen Writers Foundation, for her enthusiasm for the book and for generously giving her time and expertise to someone she had never met. I thank her and value her kindness.

Tom Elder, author, *It's All About the Timing,* for jumping right in, reading the manuscript and offering his encouragement and support, even though we had never met. I thank him deeply for his helpful persistence, but most of all for his wit and humor.

Michael Conniff, Editor, he took my rambling pages and turned them into a book. This work would not have survived without his guidance, expertise, and tolerance for a first-time author. I thank him for his patience and kindness at every turn.

My early supporters—Janet Tipton, Eva Hogan, Lauren Dailey, Lynda Davis—thank you for your encouragement and listening patience as this work took form. To John and Grace Coulter for advisement on retirement plans and life in the Philippines.

My dear friend, Judy Hill Lovins, for her extraordinary efforts to help me in every way she could without my asking and her unwavering support and assistance in this and all of my endeavors. Thank you for being helpful, generous, and kind when it counts the most.

Ken Dychtwald, Ph.D., author of sixteen books on age-related issues and President and CEO of Age Wave, a company that guides Fortune 500 companies and government groups in product and service development for boomers and mature adults. I appreciate his having faith enough in this work to write the Foreward and encouraging me to forge ahead.

Michal Brimm for her serene, soothing nature that helped me on this project from beginning to end. I thank her too for reading my first two drafts and encouraging me to continue. Her interest inspired me to go on.

Robin Bromberg, DC, my long-time friend, for reading my early work and giving me helpful suggestions on content and organization and for saying it was worth pursuing. Your time, efforts, and support are appreciated.

Steve Sand, CPA, for teaching me the difference between interest and earnings, and checking my financial information for accuracy. Thank you for saying you wished all of your clients would read this book *before* coming to your office for financial guidance.

Michele Higgs and Patty Smith for your repeated reading, honest feedback, proofreading and grammar check. You have my sincere gratitude. Melinda Clynes for sharing your expertise in marketing and editing and for being a good girlfriend.

Mary Burns, Helen Maier, and Peggy Warren, my friends for life, who have supported and encouraged me. I appreciate all that you have done to assist in this book's completion and to enhance my life throughout the years.

About The Author

Donna Davis is a new author who is approaching retirement age. She is originally from New York and is a graduate of New York Chiropractic College. She was in private practice in New York City for many years before relocating to Colorado. Ms. Davis is a skier, hiker, animal lover, and traveler. She currently lives in Snowmass Village, Colorado, with her dog, Shanti.

CPSIA information can be obtained at www.ICGtesting.com
Printed in the USA
LVOW04s1451020215

425347LV00018B/987/P